D1570679

Twayne's United States Authors Series

EDITOR OF THIS VOLUME

Warren French

A. R. Ammons

TUSAS 303

A. R. Ammons

A. R. AMMONS

By ALAN HOLDER

Hunter College of the City
University of New York

TWAYNE PUBLISHERS
A DIVISION OF G. K. HALL & CO., BOSTON

Library of Congress Cataloging in Publication Data

Holder, Alan, 1932 -
  A. R. Ammons.

  (Twayne's United States authors series ; TUSAS 303)
  Bibliography: p. 171 - 74
  Includes index.
    1.   Ammons, A. R., 1926 -   Criticism and interpretation.
PS3501.M6Z8   811'.5'4   77-25339
ISBN 0-8057-7208-1

For Barbara,
my own poet

Contents

About the Author

Alan Holder was born in Brooklyn in 1932. His A.B., M.A. and Ph.D. were all taken at Columbia University. He has taught at Columbia, the University of Vermont, the University of Southern California, and Williams College. Currently, he is a member of the English department of Hunter College, City University of New York. He is the author of *Three Voyagers in Search of Europe: A Study of Henry James, Ezra Pound and T. S. Eliot*, and has contributed articles and reviews, mainly in the field of American Literature, to a number of periodicals, including *American Quarterly, New England Quarterly, South Atlantic Quarterly, Virginia Quarterly Review, PMLA* and *American Literature*.

Preface

In 1973, A. R. Ammons received a National Book Award for his *Collected Poems 1951 - 1971*, and two years later was given the Bollingen Prize for his long poem *Sphere: The Form of a Motion*. Such recognition could hardly have been predicted from the reception, or rather nonreception, of his first volume, which had appeared in 1955. Unreviewed and virtually unbought, that book, *Ommateum*, left little or no trace of its issuance, not even in the office records of its obscure publisher. Nine years were to elapse before Ammons brought out another collection of verse, but as though to make up for that hiatus, he published four volumes in three years, one of which was the long poem *Tape for the Turn of the Year*. With that outburst in the mid-1960s, notice, mostly favorable, began to be taken of him. In time, large claims for his poetry were put forth by the well-known academic critic Harold Bloom and the influential poet-critic Richard Howard. While Ammons has not come to occupy, in the currently crowded scene of notable poets, a position comparable to that enjoyed by Robert Lowell in the 1960s (neither has anybody else, including Lowell), he has established himself as an imposing presence in the field of contemporary American verse. His *Collected Poems*, together with *Tape for the Turn of the Year*, *Sphere*, *Diversifications* and his latest volume, *The Snow Poems*, make up a considerable body of work, one which rewards close and comprehensive scrutiny. I have attempted in this study to give his canon such attention (with the exception of *The Snow Poems*, which appeared too late to be treated here).

The reader who knows anything of Ammons' work is most likely to be acquainted with some of his shorter or intermediate-size pieces. I comment on a considerable number of these, and attempt to formulate the major thematic patterns I find emerging from them. I also consider, in some detail, each of Ammons' longer poems. Taken together, these works give us a substantial, interesting, and significant way of looking at the world, usually expressed in the lively language that Ammons prizes.

We can find echoes of other poets in his verses, and I point out a number of these, mostly on a poem-by-poem basis. I have not attempted anything like a full-scale formulation of Ammons' relationships to other poets. As part of an effort to establish Emerson as the archetypal poet of America, Harold Bloom has nominated him as Ammons' most relevant predecessor, a choice to which Ammons himself has given some support. A substantial case could be made for Whitman (whose influence Ammons has also acknowledged) or Wallace Stevens. Then, too, the form of many of the shorter pieces seems to derive from the example of William Carlos Williams. But whatever other poets Ammons may call to mind, he is, finally, his own man, and both in the jagged deliveries of many of the shorter poems, and in the voluble, skittering monologues of most of the longer ones, he speaks with a distinctive and engaging voice.

The principal text for the study of Ammons' poems is *Collected Poems 1951 - 1971*. (It includes virtually all the poems of *Ommateum, Expressions of Sea Level, Corsons Inlet, Northfield Poems, Uplands* and *Briefings*.) In its table of contents, *Collected Poems* divides Ammons' work into four periods, almost all equal in length: 1951 - 1955; 1956 - 1960; 1961 - 1965; 1966 - 1971. This scheme appears to be arbitrary. Comparison of the resulting groupings with the dates and contents of Ammons' earlier volumes indicates that those volumes, taken as they stand, do not accurately reflect the order in which his poems were composed. Moreover, *Collected Poems* itself does not assure us that the order of poems within a given grouping is indeed the order of composition. As a matter of fact, there are some discrepancies between the ordering of works in *Collected Poems* and the avowedly chronological arrangement of *Selected Poems*.

Partly for this reason, I have decided not to confine my study to a volume-by-volume (or even group-by-group) approach, the procedure often followed in the survey of a poet, one based on the assumption that it will convey accurately a sense of his development. Apart from the fact that no such assumption can be made in this case, there are several crucial, on-going themes and elements in Ammons' work that a volume-by-volume approach might not highlight sufficiently. Therefore, while my second chapter does concentrate almost exclusively on *Ommateum*, which is, undeniably, early Ammons, and while my third chapter draws heavily on his next book, *Expressions of Sea Level*, I have felt free to range widely through *Collected Poems* (as well as *Tape, Sphere* and *Diversifications*) in pursuit of a particular line of thought.

As a convenience to the reader, quotations from or specific references to such of Ammons' long poems as are found in *Collected Poems* are followed in the text by the relevant page numbers. In the case of *Pray Without Ceasing,* such numbers refer to *Diversifications* and are preceded by a *D.* In quoting from *Tape* and *Sphere,* I have used *T* and *S* respectively. As a further convenience, all other Ammons poems cited in this work will be listed in the index, and followed by numbers in boldface indicating on what pages they can be found in *Collected Poems* or, when such numbers are preceded by a *D, Diversifications.*

Acknowledgments

Quotations from A. R. Ammons' works *Tape for the Turn of the Year* (1972), *Collected Poems 1951 - 1971* (1972), *Sphere; The Form of the Motion* (1974), and *Diversifications: Poems* (1975) are reprinted with the permission of the publisher, W. W. Norton & Company, Inc. New York, New York.

Chronology

1926   Archie Randolph Ammons born on February 18 in a farmhouse near Whiteville, North Carolina.

1943   Graduates from Whiteville High School. Works in shipyard.

1944 - 1946   Serves in the navy, spending some months in the South Pacific.

1946 - 1949   Attends Wake Forest College on the G.I. Bill. Receives B.S.

1949 - 1950   Marries Phyllis Plumbo. Serves as principal of a small elementary school in Hatteras, N.C. Mother dies.

1951 - 1952   Attends University of California at Berkeley.

1952   Commences twelve-year residence in Southern New Jersey, working as executive vice-president of a glass-manufacturing firm.

1955   Publishes *Ommateum.*

1964   *Expressions of Sea Level;* begins teaching at Cornell.

1965   *Corsons Inlet; Tape for the Turn of the Year.*

1966   *Northfield Poems.* Father dies.

1967   Awarded Traveling Fellowship by the American Academy of Arts and Letters.

1968   *Selected Poems.* Awarded Guggenheim Fellowship.

1970   *Uplands.*

1971   *Briefings.*

1972   *Collected Poems 1951 - 1971.*

1973   Receives a National Book Award for *Collected Poems 1951 - 1971;* granted Doctor of Letters by Wake Forest University.

1974   *Sphere: The Form of a Motion.*

1975   Receives Bollingen Prize for *Sphere; Diversifications: Poems.*

1977   *The Snow Poems.*

CHAPTER 1

Introduction

A. R. Ammons was born in 1926. He was his parents' third child, two daughters having preceded him. Of the two sons that came afterward, one died as an infant, and the other was born dead. (Ammons remembers both events.) The house in which he was born and brought up had been built by his grandfather, and was situated on the family farm near Whiteville, North Carolina.[1] The biblical echoes we get in his early poems stem, at least in part, from the prominence of the Bible in his home; indeed, it was the only book in the house.[2] Ammons attended a rural school and was let out early in the spring to help with the ploughing. Recalling his childhood as a time of privation, both economic and spiritual, he says he found compensation in "a sense of the eternal freshness of the land itself." He substituted "for normal human experience, which was unavailable to me much of the time, this sense of identity with the things around me."[3] That the self in his poems is frequently located in relation to natural objects or surroundings, and hardly at all to people, may owe something to this aspect of his childhood.

After graduating from the local high school, he worked for a while in a shipyard in Wilmington, North Carolina, installing fuel pumps in freighters. World War II was in progress, and Ammons joined the navy in 1944. He spent some months in the South Pacific, serving aboard a destroyer escort. Upon his discharge from the navy, he, like so many veterans, entered college on the G.I. Bill. Attending Wake Forest, his majors were "from time to time premed, biology, chemistry, general science."[4] This interest in science has proved a continuing one and is reflected in a number of the poems. Ammons wrote poetry at college but concealed what he wrote until a month before he received his degree. He had begun writing while in the navy, during the long periods of time between watches.

15

After getting his B.S., Ammons did some teaching, married, and served as principal in a tiny school on Cape Hatteras in North Carolina. He decided to attend graduate school at Berkeley, where he met the poet-critic Josephine Miles, whom he regards as one of the three people who have most influenced his career (the others were two of his elementary school teachers). Returning East in 1952, he settled in South Jersey, where, "after readjusting my vision to look for small things,"[5] he became fond of the land and shore (the beaches making their presence felt in several of the poems). During the twelve years he lived in New Jersey he was employed mainly by a firm that manufactured glass for laboratory equipment. He also worked in real estate and did some magazine editing.

In 1963 he went to Cornell to give a poetry reading (he had by then published *Ommateum* and *Expressions of Sea Level*). Asked by a member of the English department why he did not teach, Ammons replied "Why don't you ask me?"[6] Somebody apparently did, and he became a faculty member at Cornell in 1964, moving from instructor to full professor in seven years, and producing a body of poems that, for the most part, has been received with a good deal of critical respect.

He now lives in Ithaca with his wife and son. He teaches poetry-writing courses almost exclusively, serving at Cornell as Goldwin Smith Professor of Poetry. Ammons, then, has come a long way from his start in life as an impoverished farmboy, and from his start as a poet whose first volume, for all the attention it received, might just as well have never been published.[7]

If the world had no use for Ammons' first book, *Ommateum*, that book had only limited use for the world. Rendering its materials in a sketchy, abstract manner, *Ommateum*, the subject of Chapter 2, displays a distinct strain of alienation from earthly life, complemented by an impulse to get beyond it. Several of the book's speakers undergo a desired disappearance or dissolution, although such dissolution is sometimes involuntary and fearful. *Ommateum* occasionally directs a critical humor at its own sense of alienation or makes gesture of acceptance toward the world, but such gestures tend to be as thin and abstract as its rejections.

In the cluster of volumes coming after *Ommateum*, there is a recurrence of the transcendental impulse of that first book. But the resistance to this impulse also persists and is now firmly rooted in concrete actuality, producing more satisfying poetry. (Perhaps this rooting is a reflection of the attention to "small things" that Ammons developed during his years in South Jersey.) The tension between the pull toward the world and the pull away from it expresses itself as a dialectic between the small and the cosmic, or the temporal and the eternal, or between form and formlessness. Chapter 3 includes a consideration of this dialectic.

One way in which Ammons' endorsement of form manifests itself is in his concern with scientific materials. This concern, which is a distinctive feature of his work, is not a matter of drawing on science for metaphors, as other poets might do. Rather, the scientific references that get into his poetry reflect a real attraction to the objects and processes that concern biologists and physicists, and show as well Ammons' own scientific cast of mind. On the other hand, the force of a number of his poems comes from the manner in which a scientific apprehension is played off against nonscientific considerations, and from the amalgam of scientific terminology with other kinds of vocabulary. Ammons offers a bracing example of how the poetic mind can confront and assimilate scientific knowledge, deriving pleasure from it but at the same time maintaining a play of sensibility that goes beyond its bounds.

While science is founded on the idea of order, and while that idea certainly exerts a hold on Ammons, he is simultaneously drawn to that which eludes order, to the unpredictable and changing. The respective manifestations of order and disorder, characteristically found together in his poetry, contend for his allegiance, and he makes some effort to synthesize the two. But his sensibility is such as to resist final resolutions, here or elsewhere.

What often needs or achieves ordering in Ammons' world is motion, a quality so central for him as to be virtually synonymous with reality. It can oppress, but more often it entrances him. He sees it as at once pervasive and mysterious. Fused with an order or form, motion becomes a structured process, and it is through a variety of such processes that Ammons reverently sees our individual and collective existences being maintained. He repeatedly shows his appreciation of what Santayana called "the workshop and busy depths of nature, where a prodigious mechanism is continually supporting our life. . . ."[8] Ammons' treatments of form, science, order, and motion, all considered in Chapter 3, are sometimes expressed in meditative poems several pages in length. These come into prominence in the books after *Ommateum*, but do not displace the shorter, allegorical or fabulistic encounters featured in that first volume.

Chapter 4 considers what may well be Ammons' single greatest preoccupation, one that reflects the large abstract component of his sensibility (a component that helps give his work its distinctive flavor). This is the classical philosophical question of the One and the Many. It has to do with seeking some sort of connectedness or unity amid the diverse, discrete particulars of existence. Such a unity has been conceived of in various terms: materialistic, mystical, historical, social, moral. Ammons' conception of the problem is relatively narrow, concentrated mostly on physical things or processes (though it has some bearing for him on society, and, to a greater extent, on poetry as well). He gives the impression of an isolated mind seeking a purchase on the multifold aspects of material reality, yearning for and sometimes experiencing a sense of their coming together into a unity. But he also strongly resists such a sense, prizing variety and individuation. The idea of the One may represent an ultimate satisfaction for the abstract aspect of his imagination, but the fact of the Many repeatedly engages this poet with an eye for the small and particular, for the abundance of the world of the discrete. (Ammons has called himself "the exact / poet of the concrete *par excellence*" [S, 65.].)

We can relate the question of the One and the Many, as it figures in his work, to his considerations of order and motion. Thus, certain large configurations or associations can be seen as operating in his canon, sometimes showing up in the shortest of poems. But those configurations are largely of a dialectic; as already indicated, Ammons usually resists settling into a fixed attitude or position. His need for a sense of pattern and his love for the unpatterned and miscellaneous show up in his suggesting the existence of orders, but not, usually, an Order.

As a rule, Ammons' handling of order and motion, of the One and the Many, is done in terms of natural objects or processes, and the results tend toward the abstract. But there are also more direct, local, less theoretical encounters with nature in his poetry, and these are the subject of my fifth chapter. Indeed, one of the distinguishing marks of his work has been the reclaiming of nature as a major subject for the poet, though nature does not function for Ammons as an unfailing source of comfort or of desired significance. While it can serve to give him pleasure, it can also, in times of pain, fail him or furnish only its own instances of suffering and death. Imaginative appropriation of nature is still open to him, though the nature of nature is sometimes problematical or else the cause of apprehension.

While Ammons has written ostentatiously little in the way of critical prose, his verses often take up the subject of poetry (or the poet). At several points, his poetics, the focus of Chapter 6, intersects with his preoccupation with motion. That poetry *moves* is for him one of its central characteristics, and his repeated use of water imagery to describe how poetry operates typically presents water in motion, that is, in flow. His observations of the physical or natural world show him to be entranced by the forms or shapes that structure the motion or flow of things. But while there is an approach toward equality in his respective celebrations of form and motion, there is perhaps some tipping toward the latter; in his poetics, though he speaks of reconciling motion and shape, it is motion or flow that fascinates him, even more so than its equivalent in the physical world.

Those of Ammons' poems in which motion is least impeded, in which his consciousness is given its greatest freedom to flow, are the subject of Chapter 7. There I take up *Tape for the Turn of the Year*, *Essay on Poetics, Pray without Ceasing, Summer Session, Extremes and Moderations, Hibernaculum*, and *Sphere: The Form of a Motion*. The pieces in question (which I have designated, adapting a phrase of Ammons, as "linear modes") are his "long" works, admittedly a vague term, and one which I use to cover poems ranging from about thirteen pages to over two hundred. But even the smaller of these are long enough to permit a considerable variety of subject matter or of tone or both, leading us on a continuous zigzag. They might all be said to take as their motto (*pace* Poe) Santayana's observation that "Poetry . . . is not poetical for being short-winded or incidental, but, on the contrary, for being comprehensive and having range."[9] They seem to endorse, too, Emerson's contention in "The Poet" that "all language is vehicular and transitive, and is good, as ferries and horses are, for conveyance, not as farms and houses are, for homestead." What Ammons himself says in one of his intermediate-size pieces, "Corsons Inlet," applies nicely to these long works, namely, that he is willing "to accept / the becoming / thought, to stake off no beginnings or ends. . . ." He may sometimes speak of poetry as moving toward completion and rest, but his long poems, sprees of meditation, work against such a conception. (Though *Tape* suggests that its theme involves a coming home, it adds "and figuring out some / excuse to leave again" [T, 30].) In composing his linear modes, Ammons seems to have taken as his model the spider in one of his poems, who "spun an open-ended house. . . ." While early in his career he had sometimes feared the dissolution of the self, he is, in his linear modes, confident enough to trust to looseness, to flow. He appears to believe, with Emerson, that out of process coherence will emerge.

CHAPTER 2

A Hostile Wind

T HE poems of *Ommateum* are mostly cast as little fables
or allegories. Their isolated protagonists perform curious acts
and address themselves not to other persons, but to imposing
presences—sun, moon, wind, mountains, death. The settings are
obviously symbolic and sketchily rendered. Such few, specific
historical locales as appear are very special, exotic. Partly as the
result of all this, the poetry is personal but abstract, intense but dis-
tanced. Taken as a whole, the volume is attenuated and unduly
strange, coming to us from too far away.

I *The Dissolving Self*

Some of the poems in *Ommateum* must have suggested to what
few readers they found that this, Ammons' first volume, was in
danger of being his last. (Other early pieces, not included in that
book, could only have reinforced the suggestion had they appeared
there.) For the self of the poems repeatedly undergoes dissolution,
being overcome by its surroundings, or else bidding farewell to
them, depicting its voice as puny, futile, or silenced We seem to
have, in a number of the works, not Stevens' man whose pharynx
was bad, but a terminal case.

Ommateum's first poem begins: "So I said I am Ezra / and the
wind whipped my throat / gaming for the sounds of my voice."[1]
Richard Howard links this Ezra to the Old Testament prophet, seeing Ammons' use of the name as a desperate reaching for an
authoritative voice.[2] Like a number of other details in the early
poems, "Ezra" probably *is* intended to set up a biblical resonance.
But it hardly functions to secure the authority Howard claims Ammons is seeking. For even the modest assertion "So I said I am
Ezra," with its anecdotal locution and its naming of what might be
called a secondary (though historically important) prophet, is not
honored. As the poem proceeds, "Ezra" becomes a meaningless

21

term, falling "out of being" like the speaker it designates. The first figure, then, that Ammons chose to present in his initial volume cannot maintain his identity (calling to mind, as Harold Bloom suggests,[3] the Whitman of "As I Ebb'd with the Ocean of Life").

The *I* of *Ommateum's* next poem fares no better. He is not even permitted to name himself, managing only an "Oh." (This expression is a recurring one in early Ammons, where a principle of minimal exclamation or abbreviated apostrophe appears to be at work.) He ends up in an abject position, falling down in the dust. The wind again behaves in a hostile manner, whipping at the speaker's "carcass" (designated as such even though he is still alive).[4]

Wind is an important presence in Ammons, functioning in a number of ways, but chiefly, in the earlier poems, as a great force dissolving or belittling the speakers. At one point it is named as "Enlil," the deity of storm and a chief god in Sumerian religion. This is one of several references to Sumer in Ammons' early verse. These do not all fall into a single pattern, but the reference to Enlil, together with the poem "Sumerian,"[5] which presents a speaker "subject to floods and high winds," points up what might be called the Mesopotamian posture we find in a number of Ammons' first works. It is that of man made conscious of his own helplessness in the face of great and dangerous forces. His throat or voice in particular is threatened or minimized (see, for example, "Rack"). When, in "I Struck a Diminished Seventh," the speaker dares to assume the stance of a man awaiting inspiration, he is ignored. Then death comes, "sieving" him, that is, reducing him to sand or powder. Note, too, the oblivion that befalls the ambitious quester in "Having Been Interstellar."

The hostile forces confronting Ammons' speakers assume a socio-historical form in two of *Ommateum's* poems, "In Strasbourg in 1349" and "At Dawn in 1098." In "Strasbourg" the speaker himself is not destroyed but simply walks "out of the world." The speaker in "Dawn" performs, at least implicitly, a similar act. These two poems furnish concrete but distinctly distant contexts for their rejection of the world.

No context at all is supplied in "Some Months Ago," which is taken up with an extended farewell to objects and creatures of the earth. Rather than his own throat having been threatened or attacked, the speaker has "closed up all the natural throats of earth."

Since the world from which he has departed appears to be an attractive one, his motive in leaving it is mysterious. Not much more reason for departure from this world is given in "Turning a Moment to Say So Long." After bidding farewell to "the spoken / and seen," the speaker finds the "implicit" oppressive. Peeling off his being, he plunges into a well whose grubbiness does not prevent drowning from being attractive.

The renunciation of the world in *Ommateum* can be interpreted as a transcendental impulse rather than as a wish for mere extinction (though the two cannot be easily separated in that volume). "Whose Timeless Reach," which does not appear in *Ommateum* but is placed by Ammons among his earlier poems, employs another speaker named Ezra, who seems desirous of leaving the temporal to go out through space, "taking the Way. . . ." Given Ammons' interest in Lao Tse,[6] "the Way" might well be what it was for the Chinese philosopher, that is, Tao, the Way of ultimate reality, an understanding of which is to be striven for through mystical contemplation. But while Taoism made room for social and political applications of the Way, transcendentalism in early Ammons appears to involve putting the world completely behind him. The isolated personae of *Ommateum,* a number of whom have, like saints or hermits, removed themselves to the desert, undertake curious rituals that appear aimed at reaching the divine or eternal, and saying "so long" to this life, which is either too much or too little for them.

A concomitant of this, apparently, is saying "so long" to speech as well. The gathering of the pieces of the speaker's voice in "Rack" has as its goal the building back of "the whole silence" and "the silent offering" of his death. The visionary owl of "Doxology" is silent near death, and silence is associated in that poem with the eternal and spiritual. In "Some Months Ago" the world-deserting speaker has closed earth's natural throats. The loss of speech in *Ommateum,* then, figures both as a deprivation and as a corollary of transcendence. In this connection we should note how often the book's personae define their existence in terms of their speech, minimal as it might be. One after another quotes what he uttered on a particular occasion; the words "I said," which we find in the first line of *Ommateum's* first poem, appear repeatedly. Speech and existence are thus inextricably intertwined, and the loss or renunciation of one is accompanied by the loss or renunciation of the other.

II *The Self Returned*

If the strains of *Ommateum* traced so far were the only ones to be found therein, the volume could be seen as the expression of a sensibility deeply hopeless about and irremediably alienated from this earthly life. Both the self's dissolution and its rejection of the world operate to remove it totally from human existence. But we can find in the volume impulses that go counter to the alienation I have thus far, in effect, been stressing. For example, while "Dropping Eyelids Among the Aerial Ash" begins with an ascension that is a retreat from a world of atomic explosions, it comes to see evil and bloodshed as necessary preludes to "benefactions" and the emergence of "powers of mercy." The speaker eventually rises up from sitting amid the clouds, where he has been contemplating the world, and goes "back down into the wounds and cries," to hold up lanterns for "white nurses / moving quickly in the dark." His rising up to descend, together with the color of the nurses' uniforms in the darkness, dramatizes the poem's sense of the paradoxical compounding of good and evil in earthly life. Here, that life is accepted and endorsed. But the focus on social reality in this poem is not typical of Ammons either in *Ommateum* or in his later books. A more characteristic embrace of the world is found in "The Grass Miracles," where the satisfaction afforded by the natural is obviously very great, as it is in "I Broke a Sheaf of Light" (though expressed there with a forced naiveté).

But such satisfaction does not easily command the poet's acceptance of this world, as shown not only by some of the poems already looked at, but also by "With Ropes of Hemp." In this striking piece, the speaker, Odysseus-like, is lashed to a great oak in order to withstand a siren song, presumably addressed to his soul. He composes his own songs in praise of the rooted oak. His physically arduous and even painful position indicates the difficulty with which he maintains his connection to this world. Moreover, there is something solipsistic about his enterprise. Nevertheless, his songs to the oak do appear to have some force, giving us a figure other than the impotent, dissolving Ezra. He does "melt" at one point, but then returns. Also, rather than being like those *Ommateum* speakers who can only report what they once "*said*," he continues to "say."

There are other examples of successful assertion to be found among the personae of *Ommateum*. Neither the voices nor the actions of the book are confined to the fearful and defeated on the one hand, and the transcendental on the other. An especially interesting claim to power is put forth in "A Crippled Angel." The angel is found in a state of mourning, and, as initially presented, appears grotesque, even comic in its grief, made so by the shapeless expression of that emotion (an "agony diffuse"). The human speaker gives the angel a shaping instrument, a harp, with happy results. When the angel starts to ascend, threatening, in effect, to pass beyond human ken, its rising is dramatically thwarted by the speaker. The poem may be said to celebrate the shapeliness made possible by the operation of human limits. Not subject initially to such limits, the angel is, paradoxically, crippled. The poem arrests, in its final lines, a movement toward the infinite, thus imposing a shape upon its materials, curbing a transcendental impulse so as to arrive at something formed. (One might almost see "A Crippled Angel" as an inversion of Poe's "Israfel"—there the speaker attributes an angel's superior song to his heavenly status, while he finds his own melody constricted by the human condition.) As in "With Ropes of Hemp," power here is connected with a commitment to the earthly.[7]

The expression of the self's power and the attractions of nature and form do not constitute the only stays against the elements of *Ommateum* first considered, namely, the movement toward dissolution and the putting behind of the world. A critical humor directed at these very elements may be seen at two or three points in the book (and "A Crippled Angel" can be read in this way). "Dying in a Mirthful Place" presents a speaker who, offended by the sensuality and hilarity existing in his original location, goes off to die on a hill in Arizona, placing his head beside a great boulder. He hears buzzards sitting over him "in mournful conversations / that sounded excellent to my eternal ear." The asceticism here, in squeamish retreat from the world, is made to look ridiculous.[8] In "The Whaleboat Struck," where the speaker is killed by an arrow in the throat, marking him as a true inhabitant of *Ommateum*, his body is given over "to vultures and flies." Eventually, his spirit returns to his "Bones / lovely and white." In a wonderful, bizarre touch, Ammons has him pick up one of his ribs

> to draw figures in the sand
> till there is no roar in the ocean
> no green in the sea

till the northwind flings no waves
across the open sea
I running in and out with the waves
I singing old Devonshire airs

He is engaged in awaiting an inane impossibility, having been
prepared for his enterprise through his purification by death. The
attraction to a condition at a total remove from the world is, it
seems to me, being mocked (perhaps with some ambivalence)—note the "lovely" white bones. (Might we not have in this
a parody of the humility and asceticism of Eliot's "Ash
Wednesday," more particularly that poem's second section with its
shining bones?)

"One Composing" could be regarded as complementary to the
two poems just discussed, espousing an acceptance of the body and
an embrace of sensuality. It starts with a figure who, in an outrageous pun, is composing "seminal works" beside a brothel to
which he remains oblivious. He first delivers a languidly pretty formulation of time as futility. Having been brought a mug of stout, he
acknowledges his flesh by entering the brothel, apparently endorsing the "contemporary." The poem seems to approve the movement from the creation of his original seminal works, abstracted
from circumstances and focusing on an amorphous timelessness, to
his endorsement of the contemporary, with the succeeding genera-
tion of literal semen (though admittedly, if my interpretation is correct, the speaker's characterization of the contemporary is insuf-
ficiently set off from his original sense of time). "One Composing,"
then, comes down on the side of life rooted in time and in the flesh.

"Doxology," the longest work in *Ommateum*, appears to be Ammons' first attempt at a "big" poem. It is strange, difficult, and except for some impressive rhetoric and nicely sardonic phrasing, un-
engaging. Apart from its ambitiousness, it is of a kind Ammons has
not attempted in his succeeding volumes.

The praise of God that the title of the poem promises is con-
spicuous by its absence. Indeed, God Himself appears to be mostly
absent from the world of poem, whose chief presence is an "unconstrained fluidity," that is, a principle of change whereby men,
their religions, and their cultures disappear. Nevertheless, there is a
sense that works of art will endure, and an insistence by the speaker,
aware though he is of the smallness of his voice and its eventual extinction, on using that voice. Actually, its smallness is only alleged,
for it is capable of producing the grandly visionary or prophetic:

> You have heard it said of old time
> the streets shall flow blood, but the streets
> swept out with the flood
> shall be deposited upon sand.
> You have this word for a fulfillment.

In the face of extinction, the voice of "Doxology," at least in part, asserts its power by declaiming its fate.

III   *The Shifting Voices of* Ommateum

Ommateum's oscillations between dissolvings of the self and assertions of it, between rejection of the world and acceptance of it, make for an overall effect of indecision and fragmentation.[9] The unsigned "Foreword" to the book expresses an uneasy awareness of this and attempts to regard the book's shifts as a virtue: "While maintaining a perspective from the hub, the poet ventures out in each poem to explore one of the numberless radii of experience. The poems suggest a many-sided view of reality; an adoption of tentative, provisional attitudes, replacing the partial, unified, prejudicial, and rigid. . . ." But what sort of a "hub" is there in the volume, and just how is it related to the "many-sided view of reality"? The "Foreword" appears to find a hub, or center, desirable, and at the same time constricting.[10] Distinctly, there is an indecisiveness about *Ommateum*, perhaps reflected in its very title. The imposing, ink-horn term means "compound eye"—as in insects or spiders![11] A many-sided view of reality is one thing—the poet as bug is another. (The speaker in "Doxology" refers to himself—ironically?—as "trilobite" and "blowfly.") Ammons' title might well have offended Pope, who said: "Why has not Man a microscopic eye? / For this plain reason, Man is not a Fly."

Ommateum's indecisiveness shows up in the ways its speakers' voices occasionally shift, sometimes from poem to poem, sometimes within a given poem; at such moments the book appears to be casting about for a style. We go, for example, from the somber, Bible-echoing, prophetic or visionary mode of the first three pieces to the euphoric, false simplicity of the fourth, "I Broke a Sheaf of Light." The prophetic mode is combined jarringly with a languid aestheticism in the first section of "Doxology," and in the second section of that poem the voice seems unable to decide whether to mock or assert itself. The third section appears bent on trying three or four styles, with unfortunate results. "My Dice Are Crystal" jumps from technical specification to slangy prayer to allegorical anecdote. "I Came in a Dark Woods Upon" begins as a vigorous, comic tale, and then turns its sexual symbolism into something quite different, replete with fearful dryads and angels. "Turning a Moment to Say So Long" is out of balance in its conjoining of highly general terms with circumstantial detail (the latter a rare element in *Ommateum*).

IV   *The Wind Defied*

However shaky or uncertain his initial volume, Ammons has gone on to write prolifically. The self's dissolution has come to preoccupy him less, and in later poems where it does appear, it can be anything but morbid. In "Mansion," the speaker jauntily asks the wind, after death, to "stroll" his dust "around the plain" so he can see plant and bird. In "Definitions" the self's dissolution is lovely and triumphant, a drifting "through the / voices of coyotes," a dripping into "florets by / a mountain rock."

These two pieces point to the changed emphasis in the relationship between the self and the large presences it confronts after the earlier poems. Whether in the form of wind, mountain, or redwood, the large others are generally not as threatening as they tended to be originally. They function in a companionable way, or at least have conversational exchanges with the speaker, sometimes attempting to be helpful.[12] They have become relatively smaller, as the self has grown in stature, with the mind's power and productions celebrated (though not invariably). "Involved," for example, shows Ammons unintimidated by so imposing a phenomenon as solar radiation. He sleeps through a display of it, he himself "burning from a distant source" (this can be seen as a variation on Frost's "Desert Places," where the self's internal blankness is seen as more formidable than interstellar space).

The changed stance of the self with respect to the wind, which sweeps through so many of Ammons' poems, is especially interesting. In the earlier poems (for example, the first two pieces of *Ommateum*), the wind tends to be oppressive, dispersing, hurtful. It functions in a way closer to the wind in Eliot's "Gerontion" than to the inspiring force in the Bible or in romantic poetry (with one important exception, to be examined in Chapter 4).[13] In later poems it can still operate this way, but it can also be defied, as in "The Wind Coming Down From," which resurrects Ezra, this time listening "from terraces of mind / wind cannot reach." Wind can even be incorporated by the self. In "Reversal," the speaker, claiming to have a mountain in his head greater than the actual mountain being addressed, is charged with arrogance by the latter, who says "the wind in your days / accounts for this arrogance."[14] The significance of the poem's title may lie in the way the speaker's proud assertiveness contrasts with or reverses the wind's dispersal of the self in *Ommateum*. Happily, whatever was making for that dissolution did not prevail. As with the thawing sand of "February Beach," so with Ammons: "the dissolved reorganize[d] / to resilience."

CHAPTER 3

Forms of Motion

IN the poems of the period 1951 - 1955, Ammons displays an attraction to the condition of formlessness. He indicates that by giving up the forms of the self and of the world, one may achieve the absolute and timeless.[1] The tug toward the absolute-formless has persisted in his poetry. But it has had to contend with a distinct pull in the direction of the temporal-formed. This other attraction links up with Ammons' interest in science, which, in turn, is connected to his concern with order and that which is ordered—motion. The present chapter will take up all these matters. It will concentrate mainly on poems found in Ammons' second book, *Expressions of Sea Level*, which is particularly occupied with the issue of form versus formlessness. But that issue has been an ongoing one for Ammons, and the chapter will widen its focus to include works from later volumes.

I *The Appeal of Form*

Like *Ommateum*, *Expressions* shows signs of an urge to transcend the limits of the body, the self, and the world, to get *beyond*. But at the same time the movement toward the absolute is resisted or questioned, at least implicitly. "Hymn," for example, talks of discovering a nameless "you," which involves leaving the world. The *you* appears to be a principle of absolute being, existing outside the realm of seeing. But the poem is also drawn to the sights of earth, wishing to scrutinize even the smallest ones with "ground eyes" (that is, lenses, but perhaps also eyes for the ground). In "Requiem," the speaker rises into "singing trees," but is "massacred" by the angels associated with them. "Bourn" has its speaker travel beyond "relevance" and enter "the decimal of being," disappearing. But the poem appears to regard wistfully "the singing shores" of earth that had attempted in vain to call him back from his quest for the absolute. "Bridge" considers the possibility of spirit, "silvery with vision," breaking "loose in a high wind" and going off weightless, detached from the body. But, by making masterly use of the object named in the title, it holds up as an ideal a unity of body and spirit. "Guide" speaks of the longing for the absolute, but links that goal with death and says that in it there are "no precipitations of forms / to use like tongs against the formless." These poems, then, are at least partly committed to the temporal and material.[2]

Wind figures both in "Bridge" and "Guide," particularly the latter. The fascination wind holds for Ammons may lie in its being indubitably there, a great force, but immaterial. It is the "guide" in the poem of that name, and is credited with expertise in matters of the absolute and the formless, "having / given up everything to eternal being but / direction." Formidable in its formlessness, it is nevertheless glad to have the speaker in "Mansion" bequeath his remains to it, because "it needed all / the body / it could get / to show its motions with." (This may be read as a counterstatement to the assertion in "Whose Timeless Reach" that "The eternal will not lie / down on any temporal hill.") A similar situation occurs in "Grassy Sound," where the speaker tells the wind that he has observed its formlessness, and wishes "to know how / you manage loose to be/ so influential." The wind answers: "with grass / and read itself / on tidal creeks as on / the screens of oscilloscopes." A heron rises, opposing it, then turns and glides. The speaker professes to be dissatisfied because there has been no direct reply to his query, but he gives indication that he has indeed been answered. For it has been shown that the wind is influential, realizes itself, through its effects on grass, creek, and bird, that is, by its manifestations in the visible and tangible world. Where wind in the earlier poetry had operated to dissolve, to reduce things to its own formlessness, in "Grassy Sound" it takes on form.

The embodiment of wind within the material world is also dramatized in "Small Song," though here that embodiment seems involuntary:

> The reeds give
> way to the
>
> wind and give
> the wind away

This tiny jewel of a poem undoubtedly owes some of its power to the context furnished by the other wind pieces of the Ammons canon. But it has intrinsic force in its combination of tightness of structure and suggestiveness, and in the wonderful reversals it effects through the management of its single verb. The manner in which the initial "give" actually functions is at first camouflaged by the line-ending's fracture of "give way." What at first promises, on the basis of line 1, to be an act of imparting or handing over by the reeds, that is, their giving of something else, turns out to be a necessary bending of *themselves* before the force of the wind, this action heightened by the reversal of our expectation. Having thus created an effect of the reeds' weakness, of the small overpowered by the large, the poem, apparently about to reinforce this effect through the repetition of "give," placed again at the end of the line, sharply reverses itself, for now the reeds, in effect, act upon the wind: they reveal it. "Give" has deceived us in both its appearances, for as the poem's last word falls into place, we are shown the small, visible, and material triumphing over the large, invisible, and immaterial. Apart from the satisfaction it provides by the cunning manipulation of the simplest of language, the poem is thematically significant, linking up with other Ammons works in its conjoining of the formed and the formless, as well as in its display of a large force at work in a humble object.

If "Mansion," "Grassy Sound," and "Small Song" show the dependence of a large and formless force or entity on the relatively small and formed (through which it is incarnated), there is something of a countermovement in "Risks and Possibilities," with its Blakean assertions, for example, the "daisy / focusing dawn / inaugurates / the cosmos." The poem goes on to say that every thing is boundless, "eternal" in its effect. So the emphasis here is such that the small, humble forms are dependent for their interest, their importance, on their connection to the huge and eternal. The direction is from the small and the tangible to the large and formless. It thus appears that we have the transcendental impulse in Ammons at work in this poem, at least in a modified form. But in its concluding lines, "Risks and Possibilities" celebrates its local materials as such, that is, without setting them in a context of the cosmic or eternal. These modest identities, or forms, are finally quite good enough.

II *Variety of Forms*

Forms are not necessarily confined to the material, to tangible objects. They can be present in the mind, as in "A Symmetry of Thought," which celebrates their shapeliness and finiteness. "Discoverer," addressing someone who is going to leave "the shores of mind" for some mysterious region, urges that he carry with him various mental forms of civilization, such as mathematics. Forms can also occur in an activity. This seems to be the thrust of "Nucleus," which tells how to buy a factory, linking this, improbably enough, to Shakespeare's lines about the poet giving "to airy nothing / A local habitation and a name." The factory is described as "a nucleus, / solidification from possibility." When read this way, that is, as another work about bringing form out of formlessness, the poem seems less of an oddity than it might first appear, rightfully occupying a place in *Expressions*.

It might be added that the circumstantiality of "Nucleus," its incorporation of definite places, measurements, and times, locates the speaker in the literal, prosaic world in a way which distinguishes the poem sharply from the pieces in *Ommateum*, most of which have unspecified, symbolic, or far-removed settings. "Nucleus" appears to proceed from the poet's actual experience, as do other poems of *Expressions:* "Batsto," which tells of a car trip; "Nelly Myers," the celebration of a hired woman on the farm where Ammons grew up; "Silver," a lovely remembrance of a mule he once worked; and "Hardweed Path Going," a recollection of boyhood chores and of a favorite hog with the wonderful name of "Sparkle." These works help establish a past and a concrete existence for Ammons, confer, so to speak, a form or shape upon him (as opposed to the disembodied speakers of *Ommateum*), and so link up with the theme I have been tracing. I might note, too, that unlike *Ommateum*, in which all the poems are free constructions, several of the works in *Expressions* display, in whole or in part, stanzaic patterning. So that in his second volume Ammons is drawn, one might say, to typographical forms, among others.

"Concentrations" speaks of several kinds of forms, those of material objects, of physical activity (in which a particular entity is drawn from a large, shapeless context) and of mental activity (though the naming of this last in the poem's final phrase creates the effect of something stuck on). The opening section presents a gray, ghostly dawn scene that yields up a precipitate of particulars, mist blossoming into discreteness. The scene is people by men who "yawn out of the silver nets of dreams / and harden as entities." "Concentrations" might well remind us of Richard Wilbur's "Love Calls Us to the Things of This World." While Wilbur's poem incorporates a moral dimension absent from that of Ammons, the two works employ common terms as they celebrate the formed and earthly.

Though no instances occur in *Expressions*, we might explain Ammons' fascination with raindrops as part of his general preoccupation with forms coming out of the formless. At least a dozen of his poems refer to such drops. They are even described in terms of a "Fundamental Constant" in the poem of that name. Drops are associated by Ammons with clarity (see "Translating" and *T*, 58), and while he never treats them with the elaborateness accorded Marvell's drop of dew, they seem to represent for him a precious and precarious coming into discrete shape or form of that notoriously shapeless substance, water;[3] as such, they command his affectionate attention.

III   *The Costs of Form*

Celebrating the formed and the definite, *Expressions* acknowledges the limits of these, or to put it another way, the costs of accepting them (in one or two places, however, it shirks that acknowledgment). The primal force that is assumed to be moving through all things in "Identity" cannot be imaged and is indestructible "because created fully in no / particular form." But formed or definite things *are* destructible—perishable particles of the imperishable whole. This, I take it, is what Ammons means in "Risks and Possibilities" when, after seeing the specific objects he names as being "boundless" in their effect, he says "nevertheless, taking our identities, / we accept destruction." Reversing the emphasis of both Western and Eastern traditional religion, Ammons tells us that in dying to the eternal we are desirably born into the temporal. Meaningful life is dependent on our assumption of individual form (see "A Crippled Angel") though a consequence of that assumption is mortality.[4]

Another consequence is that of fragmentation or incompleteness. "A symmetry of thought" (in the poem of that name), that is, a mental form, is described as "broken eternity"—it has traded eternity "for temporal form." "The Strait," which pictures a priestess struggling with a god who refuses to commit himself "to the / particular," tells us that truth " 'reaches us as / fragmentation / hardened / into words.' " "Into words" suggests that Ammons sees the forms of language (and it seems safe to say poetry in particular) as intrinsically fragmented or partial with respect to expressing the truth.

This phenomenon appears to be the burden of the title poem of *Expressions of Sea Level*. It presents us with the ocean, symbolic of the eternal or "changeless," as being speechless at its center. Only at its edges or periphery does it communicate or reveal, albeit in fragments: "broken, surf things are expressions." Not at mid-ocean, but where rock and sea meet "is / hard relevance *shattered* into light" (my italics). Yet even as this poem appears to content itself with being neither out far nor in deep, with holding a "level conversation" with the sea, supposedly accepting limits to our articulated knowledge, it flirts with another possibility and may even be said to claim its realization. After telling us of the rising tide, of "wind and water motions," the poem wonders whether there is "a point of rest where / the tide turns." This is identified with a condition of "fullness" and with "a / statement perfect in its speech." As the poem concludes, it indicates that we know the large by the small: the movement of the moon is revealed by the "dry / casting of the beach worm" dissolving at the delicate touch of the rising tide.

In this conclusion we have, at one level, an apparent rejection of the point of rest (and, presumably, its accompanying fullness and perfection), because the revelation of the beach worm is that of a world in motion, one movement showing forth another. Moreover, the management of the poem's stanzas suggests a rejection of the notion of rest. "Expressions" sets up a series of five-line stanzas, in each of which a different line is indented, but in a recurring pattern: the third, the fourth, the second, the first, and the fifth, respectively. This pattern is suspended as the poem begins to speak of the rising tide that culminates in the imagined condition of rest, fullness, perfection. But the last two stanzas take up the original pattern at the point of its interruption, presumably returning us to the broken world. *At the same time*, the final lines (in what is plainly a deliberate echo of Blake), make a claim for not less than "everything" being "spoken in a dampened grain of sand." It would seem that Ammons cannot easily relinquish a hunger for connection to the whole of things (see my remarks earlier on "Risks and Possibilities"), though he bravely asserts the contrary.

A similar ambivalence shows up in "Breaks":

> From silence to silence:
> as a woods stream
> over a
> rock holding on
>
> breaks into clusters of sound
> multiple and declaring as
> leaves, each one,
>
> filling
> the continuum between leaves,
>
> I stand up,
> fracturing the equilibrium,
> hold on,
>
> my disturbing, skinny speech
> declaring
> the cosmos.

We have again the association of speech with fragmentation ("breaks," "fracturing"), and at the same time, in the bravura of the concluding lines, an assertion that the whole of things is being expressed. It may help explain the first, cryptic line of the poem to note that "silence" was seen as the mark of the changeless or eternal in "Expressions," so that Ammons may be saying his "skinny speech" breaks from but also connects back to the whole.[5]

If Ammons has shown a continuing interest in the whole of things and not just particular forms, he may also be said to have maintained a lingering concern with wind, not as something "given away" by the material world but as a formless force acting upon it. In "Project" he says that his subject is "still the wind still / difficult to / present / being invisible." In "Virtu," the wind makes a mountain move after the mountain has failed to do so by its own exertions. The wind exits from the poem triumphant in its formlessness.

IV Science

While Ammons, maintaining a connection with the formless whole of things, can echo Blake in finding "everything" spoken in a grain of sand, he can assume a most un-Blakean position in his attraction to science:

Exotic

> Science outstrips
> other modes &
> reveals more of
> the crux of the matter
> than we can calmly
> handle

The title of this, seen in connection with the first line, seems to be a pun on the euphemism for "strip teaser," that is, "exotic dancer." Apart from the joke, the title may be indicating that the assertion of the piece is an exotic or strange one for a poet to be making, naming science as the supreme cognitive mode. To be sure, Lucretius created great poetry out of an atomic theory, and, if we make the proper adjustments of the term, we can say that Dante, Milton, Goethe, Shelley, Tennyson, and Frost incorporate in their works the "science" of their respective times (or of earlier periods). Wordsworth and Whitman asserted that poetry should or could assimilate scientific discoveries.[6] But along with such hospitality there has been a distinct (if sometimes qualified) hostility to science among poets, as with Blake, Coleridge, Keats, Poe, and Yeats, or at least a decided uneasiness, as with Tennyson (and Ammons' poem can be read as taking note of such uneasiness). In our century it has been common to define the language of poetry by contrasting it with the language of science. Certainly, assigning science preeminence, as Ammons does here, has not been a characteristic response of poets over the ages, and his title appears to recognize this.

His practice of employing diction drawn from the sciences (prominent also in Robinson Jeffers) is already present in *Ommateum* (see "My Dice are Crystal" and "I Struck a Diminished Seventh," as well as an early work not included in that volume, "Chaos Staggered Up the Hill"). But *Expressions* shows that Ammons has more than a fondness for scientific terms—he has an unabashed interest in scientific materials per se. (He has rightfully been called "our Lucretius.")[7] Science does not function primarily as a source of metaphors for Ammons, but as a supplier of knowledge and concepts whose contemplation gives him pleasure. It is not a threat to him but a treasured source of subject matter. *Expressions*, together with later volumes, shows him treating materials drawn from physics, biology, physical chemistry, biophysics, geology, and meteorology. (In *Essay on Poetics* there are wholesale

quotations from scientific texts, one of them followed by the comment "isn't that beautiful" [p. 317].)

Ammons' interest in science may be seen as a corollary of his rejection of the absolute-formless in favor of the finite-formed
(though as we have seen this is not a fixed or unambivalent rejection). For science conceives of the world as a series of forms or
patterns, definable configurations. "Hymn," which registers his
simultaneous attraction to the realms of both the formless and the
formed, dramatizes his pull toward the earthly and material by its
use of scientific tools and terms: "ground eyes" (that is, lenses),
"microvilli sporangia," coelenterates." "River" may be read in a
similar way. It begins with the statement of an intention—"I
shall / go down"—to seek what might be called a "poetic,"
transcendental domain, a "great wooded silence / of
flowing / forever down the dark river / silvered at the moon-
singing of hidden birds." The lure of this timeless realm is
countered by the next section of the poem, which, significantly, is
given a specific time heading, and which presents a spring scene
marked by deliberately unlovely touches:

> the forsythia is out,
>   sprawling like
> yellow amoebae, the long
>   uneven branches—pseudo-
> podia—
>   angling on the bottom
> of air's spring-clear pool:

Notice the use of "sprawling" and "uneven," together with
"amoebae" and "pseudopodia" (see "Spring Coming"). The last
line of the stanza relieves the effect of these elements, but this
scene, with its biological terms, is clearly meant as a sharp contrast
to the one that originally drew the speaker. The poem ends with a
section that is identical to the first one, except that the initial
declaration of intention to go down to the silence and hidden birds
has now been reversed into a question: "shall I / go down." The actual, formed (if ungainly), earthly world, rendered in part by scientific terms, has made the original quest for the poetic-transcendent-
amorphous seem dubious.

As given to us by modern science, the physical cosmos is not so
much a collection of static forms, as of kinetic ones, and this is how

it shows up in Ammons' poetry. The words "mechanism" and "machine," used in conjunction with objects or beings found in nature, are honorific terms for him. "Mechanism" serves as the title for one of the poems of *Expressions*, a piece which celebrates "hemoglobin kinetics," "enzymic intricacies / of control," "gastric transformations." For Ammons "it is / wonderful / how things work" ("Identity").

He not only incorporates terms and concepts drawn from the sciences, that is, he not only presents ready-made materials, he also (and in this he is rare, if not unique, among poets) exhibits a distinctly scientific turn of mind in his own direct encounters with nature. That is, his consideration of objects can take the form of scientific curiosity and mullings, or an impulse toward measurement. In "Motion for Motion" he tells us that he might be able to say why a beetle's shadow on a stream bed is larger than the insect if he knew the diameter of the two, the stream's depth, "several / indices of refraction," etc. In *Tape* (*T*, 164), the sun's reflection on his coffee leads him to think of "the conservation of / angular momentum." He wonders, in the same poem, why there is snow only on one side of the road, and moves toward consideration of the width of the highway in relation to tree shadows (*T*, 167 - 68). Contemplating an elm tree in *Essay on Poetics*, he muses sophisticatedly on the difficulties of fixing with precision the tree's position (pp. 303 - 4).

Such passages may startle but do not make for memorable poetry. Still, the pressure of Ammons' scientific mode of apprehension can produce some notable effects, if only by being played off against nonscientific considerations. In "Cascadilla Falls," for example, Ammons is aware of the various physical motions a stone is undergoing (such as "the 800 mph earth spin") even when apparently at rest. The poem first stresses the connections between stone and poet. The stone is described as "handsized . . . / kidney-shaped, testicular," and Ammons is implicitly subject to the same variety of motions in particular directions. But while he may be rolled round with the stone, the thrust of "Cascadilla Falls" comes from its shifting of focus to the poet's difference from the stone, his lack of psychological direction. (This much may safely be said of the work, though its ending is somewhat ambiguous.)

Another poem which poses the nonscientific against the scientific is "Script," where we seem to have the flight of a bird reduced to a recording of physical dimensions:

> The blackbird takes out
> from the thicket down there
> uphill toward
> the house, shoots
> through a vacancy in the
> elm tree & bolts
> over the house:
> some circling leaves waving
> record
> size, direction, and speed.

What we see here is a delighted tribute to the blackbird, played off against the flatness of the last lines. The title, as was the case with "Exotic," can be taken as functioning in a punning way. Its significance seems to be connected with the "recording" by the leaves of the physical data of the flight. That is, in a fanciful sense, these things have been inscribed. But if we consider the bird's action, we might allow the meaning of "movie script" to the title, one which calls for a stunt, because that is what the bird has achieved, in effect, by shooting through the vacancy and bolting over the house. The concluding lines are anticlimactic, but deliberately so, by way of providing a comic contrast to the bird's spectacular burst of flight. For there is something ludicrous (and almost pathetic) about the "record" made by the leaves, when compared with the phenomenon being registered. (As *Tape* says, "the record / can't reproduce event" [*T*, 18].) The scientific notation is a stunned, prosaic response to a brilliant performance. (This poem may well owe something to Emily Dickinson's "Within my Garden rides a Bird," where a hummingbird's improbable presence is attested to by the "just vibrating Blossoms," which are pointed out by a "logician" dog.)

In "The Account" Ammons first weighs his life in terms of physics, and then considers the possibility of getting beyond those terms. He begins by wondering what difference his presence or absence on earth makes. Not "a / single electron's spin" will be lost when he is gone. But he conjectures that by spurning the earth through his mind he may ultimately triumph over a cardinal element of physics, mass. Here, then, is another instance of a poem moving past the scientific.

"The Quince Bush," one of Ammons' finest poems, shows his scientific sensibility at work in a light but crucial way. The poem presents a morning glory vine that has "run through" the bush:

> and this morning three blooms
> are open as if for all light,
> sound, and motion: their adjustment
> to light is
>
> pink, though they reach for
> stellar reds and core violets:

These are curiously ambitious blossoms, striving for inclusiveness—they are open for "all" light, etc., and reach for
"stellar" reds and "core" violets, the two adjectives suggesting, in
turn, a going high and a going deep. This would-be self-
aggrandizement is counterpointed by the dry notation, which could
only have been made by a mind of scientific bent, that the flowers'
pink color is simply an "adjustment" to light. One might also find
such a bent in the use of red and violet, the colors that mark, respectively, the two ends of the visible spectrum, and, as such, wittily
dramatize the flowers' urge for inclusiveness.

The passage contributes to the poem's central effect, its depiction
of a nature that is a refuge from the world's pain, and its
simultaneous recognition of the conflict and pain within that nature
(we are told of a "caterpillar pierced / by a wasp egg"). The morning glory finally dominates the scene but, despite its ambitious
blooms, does not obliterate the poem's sense of violence in nature or
among men. It has been put in its rightful place by the lines
quoted; their scientific sensibility serves to check any impulse
toward an unqualified, sensuous absorption in the flower, and
prepares for the final, coolly admiring treatment of the morning
glory:

> a day pours through a morning glory
> dayblossom's adequate, poised,
> available center.

Here we might take note of a remark by Wendell Berry in his
review of *Expressions*. He said that in a number of the poems "the
energy of poetry . . . takes over the language of science only as a
resource, and causes it to belong to a larger, more exuberant statement than the specialized vocabulary alone could make."[8] This
assertion does not do justice to Ammons' genuine penchant for
things scientific, nor does it cover a poem like "The Quince Bush,"
where, if my reading is correct, the scientific elements work

successfully to restrain a simple exuberance. But Berry's statement does cover the spirit of "Script," or passages like the one in "Mechanism," which, referring to a goldfinch, speaks of:

> the gastric transformations, seed
>   dissolved to acrid liquors, synthesized into
>   chirp, vitreous humor. . . .

The linking of the abstract, scientific "synthesized" and the onomatopoeic "chirp" constitutes a fine use of poetry's free hand. "Guitar Recitativos" offers another example of Ammons incorporating scientific diction into a "larger, more exuberant statement." In one of that poem's addresses to a difficult woman, he combines such diction with colloquial cant, to humorous effect. Another poem, "Miss," takes the unimaginably small cosmic particle posited by science and subjects it to a playful consonance, thereby imaginatively mastering it.

Ammons may be said to make Berry's point almost explicitly in "Translating," which describes the evolving nature of an afternoon's rain. That rain is seen with a meteorologist's eye: "several systems of / shower, the translations of heat vapor lofted to grit-ice." The drops change in quantity and size, reaching this final stage:

>   . . . I saw under the aural boughs of the elm
>   the last translation, a fine-weaving gathered by leaves,
>   augmented from tip to tip into big, lit, clear, sparse drops.

The featuring of "translating" in the poem suggests what Ammons is doing, that is, transmuting scientific observation into the language of poetry. Here, among other things, that language effects a swift, lovely incorporation of sound ("aural boughs," presumably the effect of dripping) into a scene that has been exclusively visual, and, through the assonance, caesurae, and monosyllables of the last line, renders in an almost kinesthetic way the effects of sparseness and clarity.

Ammons, then, is not hedged in by his scientific materials. He may temporarily rest within them, but can then give his language and sensibility free rein. One poem in particular, "Photosynthesis," shows how little he allows himself to be confined within the scientific given, how he can even invert that given:

> The sun's wind
> blows the fire
> green, sails the
> chloroplasts,
> lifts banks, bogs,
> boughs into flame:
> the green ash of
> yellow loss.

Here the poet produces a transformation worthy of that which occurs in the marvelous process named by the title. "Green," which
we ordinarily think of in connection with the healthy, growing, and
creative, is now turned to the end product—ashes no less—of a
destructive process, a precious quality disappearing. In its small
space, the poem puts forth a stunning reversal of the usual view.

That there has been something of the programmatic in Ammons'
use of scientific materials is indicated by his having written:

Much of what is impersonally, flatly new to us arises from scientific insight
and technological innovation. It is part of the result of a poem to per-
sonalize and familiarize, to ingest and acquaint—to bring feelings and
things into manageable relationships.
In this connection, Wordsworth's statement in the *Preface* has been my
guide and shelter: "If the time should ever come when what is now called
science, thus familiarized to men, shall be ready to put on, as it were, a
form of flesh and blood, the poet will lend his divine spirit to aid the
transfiguration, and will welcome the being thus produced, as a dear and
genuine inmate of the household of man."[9]

V   *The Large and the Small*

The scientific strain in Ammons sometimes takes the form of seeing the large in the small, or of connecting things of greatly
different dimensions. Thus, he says in *Hibernaculum* that "some
universe" comes to his yard "every day or so and bursts / into a fly"
(p. 375). This interchange of dimensions could be seen as a resolution of the tension we have noted in him, between the commitment
to the material and formed and the hankering for the absolute-
formless. But the fusing of large and small does not operate as a
point of rest in Ammons; it is at the mercy of moods, of varying
angles of apprehension. The responses in his poems to such fusions
or conjunctions vary considerably. At times we get a serious tone as

the consciousness of connection impinges on him: the "close . . . / pull between the sun and my garage snow stuns me" (*Hibernaculum*, p. 360). The seriousness can approach reverence, as in "The Shoreless Tide," which, talking of "universal principles," sees a tree's leaves registering "the slowness of huge presences."[10] But then there is the humor of "Spaceship," in which the great speed of the earth (*it* being the spaceship) somehow allows a gas can in the garage not to rattle. A mixture of tones can be found in the three stanzas of "Event," where the falling of a leaf is seen as an occurrence taking place in the universe. The first and third stanzas present this perspective solemnly, but between them we have

> worlds jiggle in
> webs, drub
> in leaf lakes,
> squiggle in
> drops of ditchwater:

This middle stanza acts to subvert the solemnity of the rest of the poem, for "jiggle," "drub," and "squiggle" constitute a lightweight, humorous set of verbs, one that shrinks the subject matter despite the expansory thrust of "worlds." Is Ammons hereby demonstrating his language's ability to subdue his formidable materials, make the amazing facts of the physical universe dance to his tune? Or is he conveying the sense that he finds absurdity in the microlife he contemplates?

Certainly, the realization of the largeness of the small does not guarantee in his poetry comforting thought about the miraculousness of it all. In "The Constant," giving us the physical dimensions of the things he sees in a seashore setting, he tells of a clam shell containing a "lake" on which there turns a "galaxy" of sand. It is a "universe" that is highly precarious, one that "a gull's toe could spill. . . ." Perhaps it is this sense of the vulnerability, of the precariousness of the large-within-the-small, that produces the weariness at the end of the poem: "I have had too much of this inexhaustible miracle: / miracle, this massive, drab constant of experience."

A sense of our *own* precariousness leaps up from the end of "World," which presents another instance of the bigness of the small registering on a viewer with a scientific cast of mind. Putting us again at the seashore, the poem speaks of depressions in the sand as "possible worlds of held water," most of which cannot outlast the ebbing of the tide. One in particular is singled out, that "keeps water through the hottest day":

> . . . animals tiny enough to be in a
>
> world there breed and dart and breathe and
> die: so we are here in this plant-created oxygen,
> drinking this sweet rain, consuming this green.

Here the bigness of the small has suddenly produced thoughts of the smallness of the big (that is, human beings), which work against the apparent assurance of the pool's continuance. (See especially the sense of precariousness in "Working Still" and "Delaware Water Gap.")

But Ammons' scientific mode of apprehension does not characteristically produce a sense of the precariousness of our state. It usually acts to confer a pleasurable interest on what he sees, or else is put at the service of an imagination that jauntily goes beyond it, examples of which we have already considered.

VI   *Resistance to the Idea of Order*

In addition to seeing how Ammons gets beyond the scientific, we should recognize the component of his sensibility that resists the scientific by undermining an essential concomitant of it, the belief in the existence of order. Not that Ammons simply eschews such a belief. He repeatedly asserts the existence of order or orders, but sometimes simultaneously points up the limits of such orders, or, even as he takes satisfaction in order, views with approval the disorder it claims to organize. In such cases, he may be said to have retained his interest in the dissolution of the self present in the *Ommateum* period (such dissolution is a return to that which is not ordered) or to have articulated that interest in another mode.

But at least one of his early poems directly prefigures the anti-order strain in him that emerges in *Expressions* and continues in later volumes. The speaker of "Chaos Staggered Up the Hill," who, in a wonderful touch, has addressed chaos as "messy," is dissolved by it. However, he tells us it has the capacity "to make us green some other place." So the principle of disorder is here regarded as creative. In his own way, Ammons, like Stevens before him, is a connoisseur of chaos.

As has been indicated, this connoisseurship is exercised within a context assuming an order. Thus, in "Motion for Motion," the deliberations on the physics of a water beetle and his shadow eventually lead to the assertion of "some changeless order extending / backward beyond the origin of earth." But before this has been affirmed, we have been told of a catbird, "selfshot," flying under a bridge. It lands momentarily, puzzling the observing Ammons, who does not know why the bird did not take advantage of a clearer route. He attributes to the bird a "will not including me." What we have here is a disjunction between man and bird and, at the same time, a similarity. For the passage on the "selfshot" bird comes immediately after Ammons has noted the gratuitous nature of his speculations on the water beetle. The bird's choice of flight path may also be seen as gratuitous. These reasonless acts of man and bird appear to exist outside the large order that the poem assumes, giving to each a particular identity, but in the poem's concluding lines that order is movingly presented as inescapable.

A bird figures similarly in "Mechanism." There the word "order" (or "orders") makes four appearances, each in a celebratory way. One example of order offered by the poem is the continuance of the goldfinch species. Yet in the bird's principal appearance what we get is not the *feeling* of order, but of its disruption, an effect of surprise, discontinuity, and disturbance, with a "hawk addled by the sudden loss of sight" of the bird.

In "Identity" Ammons takes note of the pattern or "order at the center" of the web, but seems drawn to the edges of the web where there is "disorder ripe, / entropy rich." "Rich" and "entropy" are juxtaposed again in "Corsons Inlet," where they are used to describe thousands of swallows congregating for flight in a beach setting (at the same time this assembling is seen as "not chaos"—a word more about this later). That seaside setting works, though not wholly, against the idea of order. It is a place that resists straight lines, which the poem associates with forms and fixed, ordering thoughts. The waterline itself is inexact, shifting. Ammons allows his mind to shift also—mental "lines" cannot contain the complexity and constant changes of nature that he encounters in his walk over the dunes. This is not to say he denies local orders, but he does

resist the notion of some grand order under which they can be subsumed. Around these local orders, "the looser, wider forces work."
He will seek to bring the disorder he finds into order, but he says
"there is no finality of vision" and recognizes that the dune walk he
will take the next day will bring newness, the unpredictable,
something outside any order he may set up. The freshness of disorder seems guaranteed.

"The Misfit" can be read as a spin-off from the state of mind that
produced "Corsons Inlet." Operating in a more abstract manner, it
foregoes a particular setting and focuses on the mind. It celebrates
the "unassimilable fact," that which resists being gathered into a
synthesis with other facts. Such a misfit leads us to "the boundaries / where relations loosen into chaos." It is possible that the
misfit may be made part of an order, but in the process it "dies."
On the other hand, it may triumph in its recalcitrance, and then, in
the poem's final words, it "leads us on."

In "Lines" disorder is figured not as a single, wayward fact, but,
in effect, as a large presence making up half of the poem's dualistic
domain. Charged with great energy, created partly by the heavy use
of present participles and participial adjectives, the poem pictures a
world whose "lines" are at once clustering and "weaving out into
loose ends," as centripetal and centrifugal forces pulse through it.
In an image drawn from ocean surf, the movement toward order
and the dissolution of order come together, both depicted intensely,
in a way that suggests the satisfaction Ammons takes in each:

> the breaker
> hurling into reach for shape, crashing
> out of order, the inner hollow sizzling flat:

A clear separation of order from disorder, and an unmixed
response toward one or the other, occur in only a few places in Ammons' poems. In "Laser" the mind is seized by an image that fixes
it. Finding this condition intensely oppressive, it strives to burst
"out of order. . . ." "Then One" pictures circumstances taking on
"salience" (a recurring term in Ammons and one associated with
form or order). This salience constitutes a "crushing pressure," and
the mind turns for relief to thoughts "of / things that loosen or
come apart." "Hymn V," on the other hand, wants to be assured
that God sides with order, asking (even as it seems to recognize the

futility of such a request) that provisional truth be set aside in favor
of absolute, unchanging answers. *Hibernaculum* tells us that "hell
is the meaninglessness of stringing out / events in unrelated, un-
directed sequences" (p. 361). But order and disorder in Ammons do
not typically occur in such purity or isolation. They tend to be
found together, jostling for superiority, the presence of one reliev-
ing the potentially painful pressure of the other.

"Saliences," which offers us Ammons' most extended treatment
of the theme, illustrates the dual presence of order and disorder,
even appearing to arrive at a synthesis of the two. The poem begins
with a condition similar to that of "Laser," the mind being ridden
"down / hard routes" and walled in by consistencies. But dunes
appear and provide relief. On them straight line and hardened
thought "can meet / unarranged disorder." Wind enters, not as the
stylized, destructive presence it so often is in Ammons, but literally
as wind, a creative "variable" that causes changes among the
dunes. The first of the poem's two sections ends with the celebration of the new and unexpected features that the landscape takes on
(see "Corsons Inlet").

Abruptly, the poem then provides "reassurance" that through the
changes it has celebrated there are continuities at work, making for
gradualism, controlled development: motions "do not surprise."
Ammons seems to be ignoring here the kind of surprise motion that
occurs in "Motion for Motion" or "Mechanism," and at this point
"Saliences" suffers from an Emersonian blandness. Stress is put on
what persists along the dunes, what in Ammons' sight coincides
with his memory. Then, as it moves toward a recognition of
changes, the poem focuses on disappearances, but, registering an
apparently intense awareness of mutability, Ammons softens it:

> where not a single single thing endures,
> the overall reassures,
> deaths and flights,
> shifts and sudden assaults claiming
> limited orders,
> the separate particles:

Here the limited orders are seen as subject to disruption. But
beyond those orders (which is what Ammons settled for in "Corsons
Inlet"), there is an abiding "overall" that "reassures." This last
assertion, taken alone, is grating in its glibness (heightened by the

ad hoc couplet), but gets impressively fleshed out by the poem's closing lines:

> earth brings to grief
> much in an hour that sang, leaped, swirled,
> yet keeps a round
>   quiet turning
> beyond loss or gain,
> beyond concern for the separate reach.

The movement in this passage, from the staccato and variety of mutability to the legato and unity of the permanent, conveys the feel of the belief the lines espouse. In "Saliences" as a whole, then, order, initially oppressive, gives way to rich variety. This, in turn, is seen as patterned or controlled. Next, an awareness of change is stressed, but a potentially sad sense of mutability is subsumed under the assumption of a large, if vague, ongoing order.

Resting comfortably with such an order and synthesis is not a final position in Ammons' canon. The dialectic of his sensibility is alive and well in a poem later than "Saliences," bearing the slangy title "The Put-Down Come On." At first, in this work, Ammons does seem to be resting in synthesis, saying that he chooses for his contemplation instances "where the ideas of permanence / and transience fuse in a single body," and "where what has always happened and what / has never happened before seem for an instant reconciled." (We appear, at least for the moment, to be close to the world of the *Four Quartets*.) Among the objects he mentions in this connection are ice and a slope. But as the poem moves on and adopts what might be called a geological perspective, it considers the possibility that

> . . . the slope, after maybe a thousand years, may spill
>
> and the ice have a very different look withdrawing into
> the lofts of cold. . . .

Having thus undermined the permanent (and notice how the colloquial, imprecise "maybe" works against the earlier, weighty Eliotic statements), the poem closes with the acknowledgment that at least part of the poet's time is taken up with "turning the permanent also / into the transient. . . ."

VII *Motion*

The conversion of the permanent into the transient is in accord with a sensibility that continually sees things in movement. In fact, "motion" is a favorite term of Ammons (as it is of Stevens); it occurs in the titles of at least six of his poems.[11] While in some appearances it is identified with mutability and mortality (see, for example, "Doxology" and "Ship"), it is more often made a property of treasured beings or things existing precariously—its disappearance is death or at least loss. In "Lollapalooza: 22 February," a day of thaw produces the drops that Ammons so prizes. These make a "garage-music" he listens to all day. With dusk the temperature falls, and he goes out to check: "sure enough the motions had lessened. . . / . . . the music cold-skimpy." "Viable" puts us in the world of insects and birds, where to move may be to chance death, as the opening line's pun indicates: "Motion's the dead give away." That is, motion may be the cause of loss of life, but only because it gives away or shows forth its presence. Motion and existence are virtually equated in the poem titled "Motion." In "What This Mode of Motion Said" motion is regarded as an impenetrably mysterious, all-pervasive principle of reality. While, as Hyatt Waggoner has pointed out, the poem echoes Emerson's "Brahma,"[12] it probably owes more to another Emerson poem, "The Sphinx," which mocks a poet's attempt to answer the riddle of man's existence put by the title character. In both Ammons' poem and Emerson's, reality is seen as elusive, teasing, indefinable. The metamorphoses of the Sphinx that occur at the end of Emerson's piece correspond to the principle of change named explicitly by Ammons. But the point to be made here is Ammons' linking of change to motion. His speaker, the equivalent of the Sphinx, refers to "the motions of my permanence." That which is permanent moves, or, motion is an enduring principle of existence.

With this Heraclitean sense of the world, Ammons locates order not so much in the muted movement we find at the end of "Saliences," where we have the earth's round, quiet turning, as in the maintenance of form, or pattern, within unceasing flow or change. He is attracted less by static forms than by structured processes. "Mechanism" might be considered the earliest example of this.[13] The mechanisms it praises are dynamic, the workings that maintain "a going thing." Focusing on the goldfinch, the poem celebrates "the billion operations / that stay its form." Similarly, in "Corsons Inlet," the swallows gathering for flight, while "rich with entropy," represent "an order held / in constant change." The human body, in *Extremes and Moderations,* is seen as "staying in change" (p. 334), a phrase echoed in *Hibernaculum* (p. 351). Elsewhere in this last poem, Ammons finds that earth's continuing existence comes from the fact that "our motion, our weight, our speed / are organized here like a rock" (p. 357).[14] After speaking of the carrying of genetic codes in single cells, *Hibernaculum* says

> . . . many other continuities of pattern,
> as slowed flux, work through the flux durably: adagio
>
> in furioso: a slow bass line to a treble revel. . . . (p. 365)

The poem itself is obviously revelling here in the assonance, cross-rhyme, and internal rhyme that help convey its sense of ordered motion.[15]

But as already suggested, Ammons, for all his alertness to and love of ordering principles or patterns, is simultaneously engaged by the motion or change which is ordered. (This engagement is related of course to his attraction to disorder spoken of earlier.) His fascination with flux is illustrated in a passage in *Extremes and Moderations* which still retains an allegiance to order:

> . . . if change stopped, the mechanisms of
> holding would lose their tune: current informs us,
> is the means of our temporary stay. . . . (pp. 334 - 35)

"Current" constitutes a perfect fusion of motion and order, for it denotes something that is moving and, at the same time, has shape or at least direction. In other passages Ammons tends more in the direction of motion per se. While *Hibernaculum,* as we have seen, speaks of "continuities of pattern," they are regarded only as "slowed flux,"[16] and just before this the poem states that the "metes and bounds" that things assume "break down to swim and / genesis again: that's the main motion . . ." (p. 365). "Narrows," while celebrating the forming effects of the Straits of Gibraltar, is attracted to the workings of unconstrained ocean, to "undifferentiations' wider motions." If anything is a fixture in Ammons' world, it is motion, flux. As he says in *Sphere,* "motion is our place" (S, 76), and in "The Stemless Flower," "motion . . . sway[s] all."

CHAPTER 4

One: Many

A FTER passages on the movement of cows, the nature of language, the physics of snow-laden trees, Ammons' *Essay on Poetics* announces that its subject is "one: many" (p. 300). A great number of Ammons' poems could properly make such an announcement. Indeed, the relationship of One to Many, or of unity to multiplicity, has claim to being his single largest subject. Apprehending a world full of diverse entities, the poet muses on the possible connections among them, ponders the making of a coherent whole or wholes out of reality's variegated, abundant discreteness.

I The One and the Many as a Traditional Problem

In giving as much importance to the One and the Many as he does, Ammons brings to mind Emerson, who in his essay "Plato; or, The Philosopher" saw two "cardinal facts" lying forever "at the base" of the world: "1. Unity, or Identity; and 2. Variety. . . . It is impossible to speak or to think without embracing both." Apart from Emerson, consideration of the relationship of the One to the Many has engaged a number of minds, and in one form or another this question may be said to go back to the beginnings of Western philosophy. Early Greek philosophers, such as Thales and Anaximenes, asserted the coherence of things by positing an elemental substance out of which all the world's beings and objects had been made. Anaximander, a pupil of Thales, found the basis of all things in an indefinable substance he designated as the Infinite or Boundless. The Pythagoreans appeared to believe in a divine Unity or One.[1] All these theories accepted a One, or Unity, and a Many that came out of it. Parmenides, however, posited his One as the only true being. The Many, associated with motion and change, was unreal, an illusion. Parmenides' thought was taken up in Plato's *Parmenides*, a work that served, through a misreading, as an impor-

tant source for the theories of Plotinus. He posited a formless, inef-
fable One, which he regarded as synonymous with absolute good.
Through an emanation or overflow of the One, there had emerged,
in a series of stages, all things that were. With increasing distance
from the One had come increasing division and multiplicity. The
further anything was removed from the One, the further it was from
goodness. The One and the Many were totally opposed. Existing at
the greatest distance from the One was the material universe. Man
was to strive to return to the One through mystical union, putting
away multiplicity. The One was formless, and a soul had to make
itself formless to approach it.[2]

In his magisterial study of romanticism, *Natural Supernaturalism*,
M. H. Abrams devotes a good many pages to showing how Plotinus'
treatment of the One and the Many, together with other
Neoplatonic thought, became intertwined with Christianity, and
shaped the theories of various philosophers, particularly Fichte,
Schelling, and Hegel, as well as Marx. In differing ways, human
history was conceived by them as a fall from unity and goodness
into multiplicity and evil. This fall was seen as a necessary prelude
to a circuitous journey having as its goal a return to unity, though a
higher one than that which was lost (this conception, like the next,
constitutes an important difference from Plotinus' thought).
Romantic theory typically held that in such unity "all individuation
and diversity survive. . . ." Such an ideal can be found in Coleridge, Schiller, and Hegel. Coleridge called it "multeity in unity,"
and "it served him, as it did Schiller, as the norm both for life and
for beauty. . . ."[3] Coleridge saw the history of the race as well as of
the individual as moving in a circle from the One back to the One
by way of the Many. The return to Unity in romantic thought "is
often signalized by a loving union with [a] feminine other, upon
which man finds himself thoroughly at home with himself, his
milieu, and his family of fellow men."[4] Abrams shows how such
notions of a fall from and return to unity are reflected in the poetry
not only of Coleridge, but also of Blake, Wordsworth, and Shelley,
as well as in the works of Eliot and Lawrence in our own century.

Had Abrams extended his attention to modern philosophers, he
might well have cited Alfred North Whitehead. In *Process and
Reality*, Whitehead describes the relation of God to the world in
terms of the One and the Many.[5] (Whitehead is of particular interest here because Ammons seems to have studied him at one
time.)[6] Though Whitehead gave short shrift to Coleridge in *Science*

and the Modern World, his remarks on the One and the Many seem related to Coleridge's notion of "multeity in unity."

As even this miniscule outline indicates, Ammons' concern with the One and the Many can be seen as linking up with a long line of Western thought, and he has unquestionably been aware of at least some of the thinkers involved.[7] But whatever his acquaintance with the treatment of the One and the Many in Western writings, his interest in that subject must almost certainly have been quickened by his one-time exploration of Eastern philosophy. In an interview, as already indicated, he singled out Lao Tse as one of the Chinese thinkers that he had read. Lao Tse expounded the doctrine of Tao or The Way, which refers both to the manner in which the whole world operates, and to the original or undifferentiated Reality from which the universe has evolved. A synonym for The Way is One. Thus, the concept of Tao intersects with the philosophy of Plotinus, the two furnishing part of the background of Ammons' interest in the One and the Many.

But lest I fall into the critical sin of aggrandizing my subject by simple association, I hasten to say that the One and the Many as treated in Ammons' poetry does not have the scope or grandeur that it has in Plotinus or Coleridge, or quite the conceptual complexity of Whitehead. Unlike its formulation in Hegel, say, it is not related to history (which Ammons has, by and large, not cared to bring within his poetic purview—he attempts to dispose of it in the poem "History"). Nor is it related, except in a few instances, to society, as it is by Lao Tse. No large fables or dramas are constructed by Ammons, as they are. by Shelley and Blake, in his handling of the theme. Comparatively modest in his approach, he deals with the One and the Many in short poems or briefly in longer ones. Its interest for him tends to be epistemological rather than moral or spiritual, and to be focused on the world of physical things and processes. Placed beside the writings of Coleridge and Emerson, or of other romantic figures whom he undoubtedly has read, his treatment of the theme seems comparatively narrow, specialized. But that theme has an undeniable hold on him, surfacing in poem after poem, and it takes on weight and urgency as he wrestles with it.

II   *The One and the Many as An American Problem*

Before investigating Ammons' treatment of the One and the Many, I would like to suggest that there is something in the situation of an American that may impart special force to this particular subject (and that we see reflected in Emerson and Whitman, and, perhaps less obviously, in Stevens). Our national ideals include the celebration of the individual, of his uniqueness and right to freedom. But we also espouse brotherhood and the notion of a shared American-ness, the things that bind us together. Our country encompasses great physical as well as human diversity, and yet purports to be a single nation, the *United* States of America. That is to say, our geographic and social characteristics, as well as our political principles, necessarily involve a tension, if not a contradiction, between, on the one hand, the idea of variety and individualism, and, on the other, the idea of unity. Thus, apart from the intrinsic appeal of the question of the One and the Many for the human mind, the cultural conditions of being an American may operate to give it special interest.[8]

That such is the case with Ammons is indicated in the very poem whose title points up his preoccupation with unity and multiplicity, "One: Many." The lines of this piece jump from California's features to Maine's, thereby spanning the variety of the American continent. Considering other places in America, and reminding one of Whitman, Ammons talks of "the homes . . . the citizens and their histories, / inventions, longings." He is struck by the diversity of the country, believes it to be "enriching, though unassimilable as a whole / into art" (even as he incorporates it into his verse). He finds in America "out of many, one; / from variety an over-riding unity, the expression of / variety."

In *Sphere*, Ammons again connects the One and the Many with America, saying:

> . . . I can't understand my readers:
> they complain of my abstractions as if the United States of America
> were a form of vanity: they ask why I'm so big on the
>
> one: many problem they never saw one: my readers: what do they
> expect from a man born and raised in a country whose motto is *E
> plurisbus* [sic] *unum*. . . . (S, 65).

Still, if being an American has heightened Ammons' interest in the One and the Many, in unity and multiplicity, it has done so indirectly. For this interest rarely takes the form it does in the passages just quoted. Rather, it is typically manifested in solitary musing stripped of social or cultural content.

III *Unity*

In at least two places in *Collected Poems,* unity exerts an unqualified appeal for Ammons, though the nature of that unity is not
the same in both cases. "Sphere"[9] posits the fetus in the womb as
enjoying a utopian existence. It is in a state of perfect equilibrium,
of "warm unity," in which the self possesses a universe. Being born
is a fall into multiplicity. Here, unity is a physical-psychological
condition. In "Image" it is a religious concept, one that the poem
represents as being in disrepute. Men have attempted to embody
the divine through different images, whose disappearance has
rendered the very assumption of its existence suspect, but only for
"the ignorant and stupid," who "promote the / precision of the
visibly defined." The speaker wishes that "the notion of unity could
get around," a notion that apparently involves eschewing any
attempt at constructing an image of it. For unity is indefinable and
invisible (this is reminiscent of Plotinus' One).

But it is precisely this kind of unity that Ammons rejects in
"Guide." The first two stanzas present parallel assertions: (1) "You
cannot come to unity and remain material"; and (2) "you cannot / turn around in / the Absolute." Connecting unity with death,
the poem tells us sardonically that there we will have our longing to
go back to our origins satisfied. (Just such longing manifests itself in
"Sphere," which speaks of "the dark original water.") It is the discrete entity, fallen out of unity, removed from origins, that is joined
to life: "a peachblossom blooms on a particular / tree on a particlar
day: / unity cannot do anything in particular."

For Ammons, the paradox is that what should be an ultimate
fullness, a joining together of the Many into the One, is typically
characterized by deprivation, attrition. In *Tape* he says ". . . we
can approach / unity only by the loss of things" (*T,* 23). In "Looking Over the Acreage" the conception that "all-is-one" is dismissed
by saying it is a state "where nothing is anything." *Hibernaculum*
may be said to carry this to its logical extreme, totally depriving
totality of content: "the sum of everything's nothing" (p. 379).

In these examples we find a revulsion from or dismissal of the
idea of unity being expressed through a series of explicit statements.
In other poems the attitude is not simply stated but poetically embodied. "Early Morning in Early April" ponders the scene before it,
where mist has produced an effect of glass, hanging glittering drops
in the trees:

> what to make of a mist whose characteristic
>
> is a fine manyness coming dull in a wide
> oneness: what to make of the glass
> erasures, glass: the yew's partly lost.

We have here a shift from the brilliance of the individual drops to their lusterless accumulation as mist. This is reinforced by the sound shift from the high pitch and definition of "*fine manyness*" to the low pitch and blur of "*coming dull . . . / oneness*." The scene contains shining and obscurity, as the many are transformed into the one (unity). A philosophical problem has been concretized as a visual puzzle (and aural pattern), with the poem obviously favoring the brilliant appearance of the many.

In "Staking Claim" the speaker excitedly praises the power of the mind, its ability to attain unity: "it can go up up to the ultimate / node" where opposites merge. It can go

> all the way to the final vacant core
> that brings
> things together and turns them away
>
> all the way away
> to stirless bliss!

But the celebrating voice here subverts itself. Notice, first, that the core attained is vacant. (Ammons may have had in mind The Way or Tao of Lao Tse, often designated as Nothing, in which case the first and fourth lines are punning.) Second, the recurrence and jarring juxtaposition of "way" and "away" make for strain and even ludicrousness, heightened by "stir*less* b*liss*." The attempt at climax through internal rhyme produces, in my ear anyway, an effect of anticlimax, which I regard as intentional. Also, the poem's example of opposites merging is "ascent and descent a common blip." The last word makes the joining of the two movements trivial or nonsensical. Moreover, the poem ends in a manner that further undermines its ostensible commitment to unity:

> . . . the leaves
> breaking into flocks around me taking
> my voice away
> to the far side of the hill
> and way beyond gusting down the long changes

"Way" and "away" here are operating explicitly in a direction opposite to the poem's original thrust, becoming the path to the world
of change rather than to the stirless bliss of unity.

A rejection of unity may be found as well in "Mean," assuming I
am right in my interpretation of this remarkable poem's use of
"singular":

> Some drippage and spillage in
> active situations:
> efficiency's detritus,
> fall-out from happenstance:
> a, probably calculable,
> instrank of frabigity:
> people accustomed to the wide terrain
> know, with little alarm, some
> clumps are dissolving:
> singular's the terrible view
> from which the classy gods
> take up glassy lives.

The piece begins with a laconic notation of mechanical imperfec-
tion in "active situations," which I take to be nothing less than the
ways in which the world works, operations which are "efficient,"
but that involve certain losses. These the poem seems initially to
regard with matter-of-fact acceptance. However, as in "Staking
Claim," the voice here subverts itself. Pretending to a dry, detached
tone, the poem produces a parody of detachment through the
measured phrasing and seemingly technical vocabulary of "a,
probably calculable, / instrank of frabigity." "Instrank" and
"frabigity" indeed! These, meant to sound like engineering terms,
are but nonce words amounting to nonsense (see the diction of
"Even"). The poem gives its true feelings away when it refers to the
"terrible view" of the gods. What Ammons is speaking of here, I
believe, is the gods' perception of the totality of things as con-
stituting a unity—this accounts for the use of "singular" (which I
also take to have a sardonic connotation, namely, "remarkable").
This privileged perception of unity (shared by "people accustomed
to the wide terrain"—see the "wide oneness" of "Early Morning in
Early April"), is the view from afar. The gods presumably think in
terms of the "mean," or average, of the totality. Close up, there is
the fate of the parts that go to make up the whole, parts regarded
simply as dissolving clumps. The discrepancy between the status of

such clumps and that of the gods is immense, and bitterly rendered by the jarring cross-rhyme of "classy" and "glassy" (the latter term probably meant to suggest "hard, removed"—see "Glass"). In "Mean" the sense of how the universe operates is comparable to that in Epistle I of *Essay on Man*, but without the essential element of Pope's acceptance. The poem is much closer to Emily Dickinson bitterly watching a flower "beheaded" at play through the ordering operations of a nature watched over by an approving God. Unity, in "Mean," is associated with divine meanness or heartlessness.

If "Staking Claim" and "Mean" see the apprehension of unity as available to at least some people, other Ammons poems look upon such a state of mind as unattainable. In "Corsons Inlet" Ammons finds that he is capable of discerning local coherences "but Overall is beyond me." In this poem he is made glad by his limitation. But in the opening stanzas of *Essay on Poetics* (p. 296) he seems at least somewhat rueful that the wholeness he can achieve in lyric poems encompasses only limited materials. Both here and in "Corsons Inlet" there is a fatalism about the limits of mind in bringing the world's diversity into unity. The opening of "Russet Gold" might also be read in this way. Ammons seems to be saying there that he does not expect to receive a vision of the coming together of things. Satisfaction must be found in contemplating humble, individual items, such as drops on a piece of cellophane, bark loosening "on a soggy stick."

IV *Multiplicity*

Drops and bark are in the domain of multiplicity and discreteness. This need not be regarded merely as something that has to be settled for when the approach to unity fails. Rather, multiplicity is often seen as precious in Ammons (a corollary of his attitude toward form, for the realm of the multiple and the realm of forms are identical).

A poem in *Ommateum* may be regarded as foreshadowing this prizing of multiplicity. Looked at in such a way, "In the Wind My Rescue Is" falls into place in the Ammons canon, whereas in the context of that first volume alone, it is something of an anomaly. How could the wind, so dangerous in early Ammons, function as a rescuing agent?[10] It operates as such by providing "the seed safety / of multiple origins." In so doing, it works against the speaker's self-appointed task of constructing an edifice out of stones of the earth, gathering them "into *one* place" (my italics). That is, an impulse toward building an imposing unified structure, a static entity, is happily checked by a force connected with looseness, movement, and multiplicity.[11]

The wind may be said to function in a related way in "Saliences," where it is a "variable" making for changes in the dunes setting of the poem. The resulting multiplicity is linked to freedom of the imagination. Freedom and multiplicity are also joined in "One: Many," though here it is the "freedom of each event to occur as itself." That is to say, multiplicity is related to, if not equated with, an open-ended universe capable of generating unique occurrences, unconstrained by an *a priori* pattern (see the ending of Stevens' "Sunday Morning"). While "One:Many" talks of keeping both one and many in operation (as do Coleridge and Whitehead), it seems primarily concerned with avoiding formulations that impose unity by destroying diversity. Such formulations lack richness and constitute thin abstractions.

A similar view shows up in *Tape*, which speaks of "the inexhaustible / multiplicity & possibility / of the surface," as opposed to the "depths," which are conceived of as a "few / soluble drives, / interesting, but to be / returned from" (p. 13). Here there is not a single unity in question, but a series of unities (including, say, the notion of the unconscious). Nevertheless, the enchantment with the variegatedness of phenomena, rather than with the abstract formulations that attempt to organize or fuse them, is obviously close to the slant of "One:Many." In "Celestial" the multiplicity of the mundane calls forth Ammons' affection. Beautiful dusk scenes are regarded as partly composed of the "mean and manyful," and the poem ends with praise of the multitudinous and ordinary, the "millions whose / creation was superb, if not special."

V *Ascents and Descents*

The attraction to unity and the counterpull of multiplicity are related to and sometimes directly dramatized by Ammons' use of ascents to and descents from allegorical or symbolic heights. While occurring mostly in the volumes after *Corsons Inlet* and *Tape*, this device came to him early in his career, judging by the placement of "Choice" in *Collected Poems*. Confronting the speaker in that work is a stairwell with golden steps leading upward and dark steps going down. The upward path is linked (like unity) to the immaterial.

Such a connection, that is, between ascent or height and the immaterial, appears repeatedly in the poems. (The complementary connection joins descent and the material.) The speaker of "Look for My White Self," a purged, cleansed being, a ghost, associates himself with a mountain, a "height of snow." The spirit in "Bridge" climbs "higher and higher / toward the peak no one reaches live." A poem that speaks of "the world beyond," which "burns dimension out of shape," is called "Peak." In "Loft" the title refers to a level of perception akin to "abstractions's gilded loft" occupied by the speaker in "Levitation," who is investigating "the / coming together of things" (an explicit linking of height and the quest for unity). "The Unmirroring Peak" speaks of "the highest heights" achieved by mind, where all is "immaterial."

We might say that the decision in "Choice," to descend the dark steps rather than ascend the golden ones, prefigures several rejections in Ammons of the climb to height. "Peak," for example, seems to reject "the world beyond," and chooses, though somewhat ambiguously, "the apple," symbolic of this world. Two other rejections of height occur in poems which employ a device used throughout Ammons' works, namely, a verbal exchange between a human speaker and inanimate object. In one, "Mountain Talk," when asked by the mountain whether he really wants to share its "unalterable view," the speaker goes on counting his "numberless fingers," a not very felicitous image that seems to amount to an endorsement of multiplicity, as opposed to the oneness of the mountain's prospect (see "Height"). In "Kind," mocked by a giant redwood glorying in its " height and distant view," the speaker defends his preference for weeds and "stooping" (the poem may owe something to Emerson's poem "Fable"). This is similar to the use of height and weeds in "High and Low," where the speaker, dissatisfied with his ascent to a mountain risen within him

> rubbled
> down the slopes to
> small rock
> and scattered weed.

The conversion of "rubble" to a verb nicely initiates the descent to modest and nondescript multiplicity, to disorder ("*scattered weed*"). "Convergence," which follows immediately on "High and Low" in *Collected Poems*, also deals with climbing a symbolic height, this one representing a "joining" of the speaker's sorrows (so suggesting, like the title, a kind of unity). But the position gained is made dubious, being described as "the peak of / illusion's pyramid," which suggests something other than a peak in Darien. In "Reward" the title refers to what is earned by a hard climb to a peak, namely, that "the / major portion of the view was / descent."

Moreoever, the "gain" through ascent that we find in "Offset," a poem which carries no suggestion of a subsequent descent, causes us to question it. That gain is described as "extreme & invisible"; "the eye / seeing nothing / lost its / separation," and "self-song / . . . became continuum." The self, or its song, has become indistinguishable from its surroundings. It may be said to have achieved unity. In this reworking of the theme of the self's dissolution, Ammons reminds us of Emerson in his famous "eyeball" passage in *Nature*. There Emerson says that in the woods he feels "uplifted into infinite space,—all mean egotism vanishes. I become a transparent eyeball; I am nothing; I see all; the currents of the Universal Being circulate through me; I am part or parcel of God." Emerson's seeing all while Ammons sees nothing may not be an absolute difference; remember Ammons saying that "the sum of everything's nothing." But where Emerson regards his experience as a supremely privileged moment, Ammons, it seems to me, is troubled by the loss of self in its experience of height and unity. Notice the striking fate of the quester in "Separations"; ascending a white mountain, he perishes, "swilling purity."

"One More Time"—the title might well be acknowledging Ammons' fondness for employing symbolic heights—talks of going to "high" places where there is a reduction "to rock, the single substance." That this is related to the perception of unity is clear when the one choice open at the heights, namely, going down, results in a coming upon "deepening multiplicity, / trifling, discrete abundance, / bottomless diversity." The poem obviously values the variety attendant upon descent, endowing it with the paradoxical quality of being at once trifling and bottomless.

But of course the recurrence of heights in Ammons suggests an ongoing urge to scale them, or, we can say, ascend to unity. The purified speaker of "Look for My White Self" pictures himself as "singing" at a height of snow. Experiencing a seizure of height, the man in "Moment" feels he is undergoing a destruction that is "blessed." The "bodiless loft" in "Loft" places the speaker "above the level of most / perception," and in "Levitation" the investigator of the "coming together of things" may be cramped, even endangered, by his abstractions, but enjoys his triumph over the ground's downward pull, its persistent, would-be reductiveness, emphasized by the poem's rhymes. The sojourner among the elemental presences of height in "Cougar" does not want to forego them. Attaching an heroic air to his enterprise, the poem is similar to Stevens' "How to Live. What to Do," with its two climbers who come upon an "heroic height." *Tape* identifies poets with peaks, albeit "peaks of need," who release "cold / majesties," and are "cut off / from the common / stabilizing ground of their / admirers" (p. 130). "The Unmirroring Peak," describing the constantly changing world by what might be called disrespectful syntax, plainly celebrates the height above change achievable by the mind.

Height, while sometimes representing an undesirable remove from the material and multiple, cannot be refused or retreated from without some misgivings. The point is made through Ammons' nice appropriation of two clichés in "Cleavage":

Soon	as
you	stop
having	trouble
getting	down
to	earth
you	start
having	trouble
getting	off
the	ground

The cleavage here is not just present in the typography, but in Ammons' attitude toward heights and low places, unity and multiplicity. (His ambivalence was dramatized relatively early in his career in "Hymn," which spoke at once of leaving earth to go up "into the . . . undifferentiated empty stark" [unity] and staying on earth "with the separate leaves" [multiplicity].)[12]

VI   *High* and *Low*

In perhaps a dozen of the poems, height, or at least some form of upward movement, *combines* with lowness or descent to figure in an important way different from those we have been considering. The simultaneous presence of the two placements or movements

signals experiences or conditions or moments of particular felicity
for Ammons. In "Choice," having selected the *descending* steps of
the staircase, the speaker achieves "high purity." "Bridge," which
symbolizes an ideal combination of body and spirit through a bridge
arching over a pond, renders reflections in the water by saying
"people / rising on the bridge / descend into the pond." "Open,"
celebrating sexual pleasure, presents the human body in terms of
"magnified territories of going down / and rising." These examples
all involve human activity. Other combinations of ascent and descent, highness and lowness, are seen in nature. In "Locus," a tree
with winter-burnished leaves that has been transfigured from a
"ruin . . . to / stillest shining," is introduced in this way: "the
small oak / *down* in the / hollow is / lit *up*" (my italics). "Ad-
mission," coming immediately after "Locus" in *Collected Poems*,
and intimating the possibility of some sort of transcendence, begins:
"The wind high along the headland, / mosquitoes keep low."
Celebrating light, "The City Limits" notes that "birds' bones make
no awful noise against the light but / lie low in the light as in a high
testimony." (For a poem that echoes the language here but *splits*
high and low, see "Tussock.") The human and the natural combine
to form a high-low pattern in "Ground Tide," where Ammons, experiencing euphoria while riding over a series of ascents and
descents, talks of easing out "into the open / failing slopes, led by
the spiritual, risen stream." In "Definitions," telling us "The weed
bends / down and / becomes a bird," Ammons says "I / have got
my / interest up in / leaf / transparencies," going on to see an attractive dispersal of himself in nature. Such fusions of high and low,
or ascent and descent, are obviously of great significance to Ammons, self-contained entities not subject to the ongoing dialectic
that characterizes consideration of the One and the Many in his
poetry (though as we shall see in Chapter 7 there is one poem, *Pray
Without Ceasing,* in which Ammons questions his attraction to
high-low fusions).

VII   *Center and Periphery*

The figures of "center" and "periphery" are as prominent in the
poems as those of ascent (height) and descent (lowness). The two
sets of figures can be shown to be related if we keep in mind that
Ammons associates unity with order, multiplicity with disorder. (In
a few poems—"Kind," "Meteorology," "One More Time," and

Essay on Poetics—the height and periphery figures actually intersect.)[13] "Identity," using a spider web as its starting point, clearly identifies the center of the web with order, its periphery with disorder. "The Misfit," celebrating the fact unassimilable into theory, places such a fact at "the edge" or boundaries, which the "nucleus," or center, "fails to control." A passage in *Tape*, after linking order and center, joins multiplicity to periphery and, implicitly, to disorder (p. 113).[14] This connection of multiplicity and periphery is effected again in the poem entitled "Periphery," and complementing it is the joining of center and unity. The quest for essential truth in "The Arc Inside and Out" is rendered in terms of stripping away peripheries and coming to a center of "oneness."

Just as unity sometimes figures as something difficult, perhaps even impossible to reach, so does center. The sea in "Expressions of Sea Level" speaks to us "far from its center." Only its edges are articulate and visible—the first word of the poem, noting the action at those edges, is "Peripherally."[15] "Meteorology" advises us to confine the self to " 'extremities & superfices' / the unenterable core's rusty / lode shut up." *Hibernaculum* tells us that the poet's hope that he can find in a "central / core's center the primordial egg of truth" is an illusion (p. 372). The setting sun of "Left" is treated as the center of the dome of the sky, which is "inscrutable by clarity / & undifferentiation." This phrase, somewhat inscrutable in itself, may be said to receive amplification and explication by the next (and final) poem of *Collected Poems*, "The Arc Inside and Out." This work indicates that one possible way to unity would involve the elimination of reality's superficial data, possibly producing a "distilled / form." This I take to correspond to the "clarity" in "Left." The second path to unity, "Arc" suggests, would be through inclusiveness, a conceptual shoveling together of the world's abundance, "plenitude / brought to center. . . ." This may be said to correspond to "undifferentiation" in "Left." "Arc" sees neither method as working, for, as in *Hibernaculum*, the hope of reaching center is an illusion.[16] The very poem entitled "Center" points up the elusiveness of that entity:

> A bird fills up the
> streamside bush
> with wasteful song,
> capsizes waterfall,
> mill run, and

> superhighway
> to
> song's improvident
> center
> lost in the green
> bush green
> answering bush:
> wind varies:
> the noon sun casts
> mesh refractions
> on the stream's amber
> bottom
> and nothing at all gets,
> nothing gets
> caught at all.

Note that the effect of the song is at first disordering ("capsizes")
and then organizing, with the objects named in lines 4 - 6 ap-
proaching the song's center. But that center is lost in a bush oddly
separated from its color, that coming apart countering the
preceding centrifugal movement (indeed the lines about the bush
are so written as to require, as is often the case with Ammons, an act
of taking apart by the reader). Moreover, instead of a clear, unifying
center, we get a sense of multiplicity, through the varying action of
the wind (see "Saliences"). There is a further effect of what might
be called uncentering in the construction of the last three lines.
Coming up against a surprising comma (one would expect no break
after "gets"), the reader is momentarily tempted to regard "noon
sun" as the subject of "gets," with that verb operating as parallel to
"casts." That is, the sun casts but gets nothing at all. As it turns out,
"gets" is actually functioning as an auxiliary verb, taking "nothing"
as its subject. But the essential meaning is not changed by the cor-
rected reading. For when we get the lines straightened out, we are
still left with "nothing." A center may be said to exist but cannot be
grasped.

Baffled in the quest for center, we are left with periphery. But as
with multiplicity, Ammons does not necessarily regard location
there simply as a matter of deprivation. In "Square" he claims "The
formulation that / saves damns"[17] and declares himself a
"periphery riffler." The gayly ostentatious play of sounds in this last
phrase would appear to indicate that Ammons takes satisfaction in
being away from a clarifying center, the saving-damning formula-

tion (though he cagily does not get too far away). He is content to root about in that which cannot be formulated, the "riddling underbrush."[18] In the piece entitled "Periphery," he begins by complaining about such terrain, difficult "thickets." Periphery is linked to multiplicity here, the latter regarded as a host of precise, discrete phenomena but leading only to crude conclusions. Deciding to penetrate toward the center (that is, presumably, toward a more satisfying form of truth), he hesitates, and is rewarded:

> . . . I came on a spruce
>
> thicket full of elk, gushy snow-weed,
> nine species of lichen, four pure white
>   rocks and
> several swatches of verbena near bloom.

The reward is precisely the multiplicity (nine species!) he originally found unsatisfactory. The strong *k, sh* and *ch* sounds here adds to the effect of the thicket's richness.

But periphery cannot always content. It is associated in "Locus" with an oppressive sense of time's passage, and, in *Essay on Poetics*, with the dangerous possibilities of chance and "entropy" (p. 316) that at other times engage Ammons. Periphery can also mean the superficial for him (see *Essay on Poetics*, p. 312), and in "Object" he berates himself for being too ready to accept it:

> X out the rondure of
> the totally satisfying
> and all other sizable areas
> near the central scope:
> that degree, that circumference,
> put aside: the leftovers,
> though, pips & squeaks,
> think to pick up, shovel
> up, if possible: that is what
> is left: stuffing the central
> experience into the peripheral
> bit overinvests though &
> creates aura,
> wistfulness and small floating.

Starting here with the self-admonition to eliminate the center, he ends up by regarding the subsequent absorption with the peripheral as an overvaluation leading only to minor apprehensions.[19]

VIII   *Polar Clusters*

Drawing together the elements discussed in this chapter, as well as some of those treated in Chapter 3, it is possible to set up two groups or clusters that may be said to constitute the poles between which Ammons' sensibility oscillates:

One (Unity)	Many (Multiplicity)
formlessness	form
order	disorder (entropy)
stasis	motion
height	ground level
center	periphery[20]

The respective conjunctions of formlessness and order, form and disorder, may seem peculiar, but I believe the basis for these joinings has already been furnished. To summarize this point, formlessness is the quality of the overall order, of the One, while form is the quality of each of the discrete entities making up the Many, entities whose separate beings are not gathered up into an order, but exist in disorder.

While the above bipolar scheme is, I believe, valid as far as it goes, there is something within the body of Ammons' poems which makes necessary a supplement to that scheme. He is concerned not only with the form, say, of a raindrop, but also with form in a more abstract sense, for example, that of a physical law which governs the behavior of individual entities. There is in him the impulse to find or contemplate such forms, which may figure as ascents to a height, or penetrations to a center, *without* going all the way to total Unity. There are, then, two ways of regarding the relationship of the One to the Many in Ammons, which can be illustrated as follows:[21]

I   the world as
    a totality

      One (Unity—formlessness,
        order)

II   a particular aspect
    of the world

      One (Form—a specific
        pattern governing
        a selection from
        the Many)

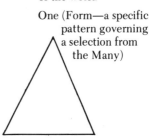

    Many (Multiplicity of discrete
      forms, disorder)

    Many (Multiplicity of dis
      crete forms, disorder)

But even within the limits of the second scheme, Ammons exhibits the oscillation, the dialectical movement present between the One and Many clusters originally designated. He is attracted now to disorder or discrete entities, now to pattern. "Saliences," which, as already noted, moves from an emphasis on multiplicity to one on order, uses its title word to designate approvingly both the individual features of landscape *and* the forms that those features assume. In *Tape* the attraction both to the individual entities and to the forms arising from them shows itself plainly. The poem notes that "facts get lost" in an hypothesis, "while one fact/ or two,/ . . . can't make a meaning" (*T*, 176). In *Essay on Poetics* Ammons tells us "I proceed a little way into similarity and / withdraw a bit into differentiae" (p. 302), which is another way of saying he alternates between a quest for pattern or form and a regress into unordered discreteness. In the same poem he talks of celebrating both unity and multiplicity (p. 304), and states, in an unabashedly prosy passage:

> . . . the mere massive pile-up of information
>
> is recalcitrant to higher assimilations without great loss of
> concretion, without wide application of averaging: things are
> reduced into knowledge: and truth, as some kind of lofty reification,
>
> is so great a reduction it is vanished through by spirit only. . . .

When this happens, "The mind searches its culture clutch for meaningful / or recurrent objects" (p. 308). We might note the use

of the words "higher" and "lofty," an example of the association in
Ammons of height and the search for form, in the sense represented
by the second triangle above. The traditionally honorific content of
these terms is here undermined by Ammons' unease with the
abstraction involved, the remove from the particular. At the same
time, he feels the need for at least limited forms—"recurrent objects." But in the same poem he seems to point to the possible
dangers even of these. Speaking of oneness in connection with both
social organization and poems, he says "oneness is / not useful
when easily derived . . . manyness is not truthful when / thinly
selective" (p. 315). At first appearing to be set in balanced antithesis, these statements are actually complementary, both coming
down on the side of a large, rich multiplicity. Yet in *Extremes and
Moderations* Ammons finds that diversity "is not ever-pleasing,"
and cites an example of his interest being commanded by the form
an aggregate of fine particulars took, rather than by the particulars
themselves. The poem strongly rejects those who cannot rise above
the concrete (p. 329).

IX   *Search for Synthesis*

Drawn now to the One, now to the Many, Ammons repeatedly
seeks (especially in *Tape* and *Essay on Poetics*) for a mode of synthesis, a vantage point that will take adequate account of both. In
"One: Many" he explicitly sets up such a goal: "To maintain
balance / between one and many by / keeping in operation both
one and many" (p. 138). This poem seems primarily interested in
cautioning against a unity that is achieved through destruction of
diversity. But at the end of the poem, he says, rather too easily, that
events (the operation of multiplicity) take on "inevitable balances."
What started out as a presumably difficult task for consciousness—"To maintain balance etc."—has been displaced by
something that is done for us, something that simply happens. A
solution, then, to the problem of the One and the Many is merely to
assume that the two are reconciled or synthesized in the course of
events. Similarly, *Tape* asserts that "high entropy / is not loss of
pattern" (p. 123), and that unity may "afford the / individual / more comfortably than / division could" (p. 186). But
these statements of reconciliation or synthesis are simply assertions,
unearned. In the same vein, *Tape* also says that reality can go in
many ways at many levels and still display "discernible unity" (p.

165). For a moment the poem seems to question what it has said, as an arbitrary imposition of order, but then focuses on a reconciliation of the One and the Many.

Not given to easy or sweeping solutions, but offering partial, limited reconciliations, are those passages in Ammons which suggest synthesis through what might be called many onenesses, or a multiplicity of unities. These are related to, and overlap with, the limited forms spoken of earlier. Ammons, in such passages, is in effect admitting, like Stevens, that he cannot bring a world quite round. Thus, despite its apparently pretentious title, "The Unifying Principle" turns out to be troubled and modest. Untypically concerned with welding a social unity out of diverse individuals, it offers us not *the* principle, but a series of possible principles, or rather, objects, for example, "a / phrase shared, an old cedar long known." *Essay on Poetics*, after announcing that its subject is "one: many," speaks of the

> mechanisms physical, physiological, epistemological, electrical,
>
> chemical, esthetic, social, religious by which many, kept
> discrete as many, expresses itself into the
> manageable rafters of salience, lofts to comprehension, breaks
>
> out in hard, highly informed suasions, the "gathering
> in the sky" so to speak, the trove of mind, tested
> experience, the only place there is to stay, where the saints
>
> are known to share accord and wine, and magical humor floats
> upon the ambient sorrow: much is nearly stable there,
> residencies perpetual, more than less. . . . (p. 300)

The initial profusion of adjectives itself creates a sense of the many that the passage wants to preserve, even as it talks of climbing the heights to understanding ("rafters," "lofts," "highly informed"), the discovery of unities or patterns. Also, in the country of the mind made up of such patterns, we notice that "stable" and "perpetual" are both qualified. Moreover, on the page before this passage, Ammons has converted "center," usually synonymous with unity or the One, into a term eliminating the notion that there exists *the* center: "reality is abob with centers: indeed, there is / nothing but centers" ([p. 299]; this is reminiscent of Whitman's statement in *Song of Myself* that "there is no object so soft but it makes a hub for the wheel'd universe"). *Tape*, which can talk too easily of unity, also contains lines that emphasize a plurality of centers, calling for their proliferation (*T*, 116).[22]

That poem connects such centers to motion, and *we* can connect what I have called the multiplicity of unities in Ammons to the patterns within motion spoken of near the closing of the preceding chapter. Any such pattern may be said to constitute *a* unity for Ammons, so long as its rootedness in motion and its limited nature are kept in view. Such would seem to be what he is suggesting in the opening of *Hibernaculum*, with its linking of motion, form, center, and periphery:

> A cud's a locus in time, a staying change, moving
> but holding through motions timeless relations,
> as of center to periphery, core-thought to consideration;
>
> not especially, I'd say, goal-directed, more
> a slime-and sublime-filled coasting, a repeating of
> gently repeating motions, blissful slobber-spun webs. . . . (p. 351)

The offering of the chewing of a cud as an example of "timeless relations" is a deliberate and wonderful indulgence in the outrageous. This yoking together of slime and the sublime is a piece of play, Ammons treating his philosophical preoccupations humorously, to produce what is primarily a charming *tour de force*, but one that points up the interrelationship of some of his key concepts.

At one point in *Hibernaculum*, Ammons appears to grow impatient with two of those concepts. After tracing movement back and forth between center and periphery, the poem dismisses them as "two nothings" (p. 373). The passage in question speaks of "tangles," and is itself somewhat tangled and inconsistent, but despite its narrow focus (it is discussing the poet's activity versus the critic's activity), it distinctly appears to move toward what seems a general nihilism, this stance displacing the question of reconciling center and periphery.

That passage can be thought of as a precursor of the final poem of *Collected Poems*, "The Arc Inside and Out." For *Hibernaculum* associates center and periphery, its "two nothings," with "impoverishment" and "abundance," respectively. These are echoed in the characterization in "Arc" of the two possible ways, noted earlier, of handling the problem of the One and the Many. The first, the casting off of peripheries, would result in an "im-

poverished diamond," while the second, the piling up of the world's
diversity, would constitute a "heterogeneous abundance / starved
into oneness." Either approach is seen as a passage to nothing.
What "Arc" does is to forego the problem of reconciling the One
and the Many, of penetrating to center or strenuously investigating
periphery. It takes on a nihilistic view but not a dismal one, settling
for an arc, that is, existence in a physical world, gratifying to our
senses. Within or without the arc there is only nothing.[23] It is as
though Ammons has become fatigued by the rigors of wrestling
with unity and multiplicity, and is throwing off wearying consciousness, willing himself into simplicity and enjoyment. He does
not wish to leave the arc, to go inside it or outside it:

> . . . neither way to go's to stay, stay
> here, the apple an apple with its own hue
> or streak, the drink of water, the drink,
>
> the falling into sleep, restfully ever the
> falling into sleep, dream, dream, and
> every morning the sun comes, the sun.

The domain depicted is like the one we get in Stevens' "Sunday
Morning," without the central awareness of death. While we may
resist this retreat into the sensory, it is rendered in a striking way,
the repetitions making for cadences untypically passionate and
seductively lovely.

   In *Diversifications*, in the third of "Three Travelogues," which
describes a walk along a woods' edge, Ammons again takes up the
quest for the One, in the form of center. This time, in a magical moment, involving the kind of ideal high-low fusion spoken of earlier,
but which is now related to the question of the One and the Many
rather than transcending it, Ammons comes to center after
meandering through "margins" (periphery) and multiplicity. He
does so not through the effort he expends, but by hearing from
flawed and broken elements, "a branch-trickle whose small
music / . . . brought the world / whole and full again and to
itself."

CHAPTER 5

Plundering Stranger

AMMONS' scientific sensibility and his preoccupation with the One and the Many frequently make for abstract and idiosyncratic musings on the natural world. But his poetry also contains numerous considerations of nature that operate in a less theoretical and special way. These partake more of the sensory and emotional than of the biological or philosophical, sometimes linking up with the works of various poets of the last two centuries. The poems which illustrate this side of Ammons (a few of which have been examined earlier in other connections) are the subject of the present chapter.

I *Nature as a Source of Pleasure*

Sometimes, whether in forest, field, at the shore, or in his own backyard, Ammons looks on nature with absorbed delight. Even amid the largely alienated early poems, we can find instances of this. "The Grass Miracles," whose dreamy unhurriedness reminds one of Keats's representation of autumn, describes an immersion in the season's richness, a

> bending to part the grass
> to what round fruit
> becoming entangled in clusters
> tying all the future up
> in variations on present miracles

The unspecified fruit and the interrogative phrasing designating it convey a sense of abundance and possibility. The syntactical ambiguity of the second participial clause—is it the fruit or the speaker who is becoming entangled?—works to mesh the human and the natural.

74

Another early example of pleasurable contemplation of Nature is "Bees Stopped." The mode of this is quite different from that of "The Grass Miracles." Nature, more dynamic here, is presented in a brisk, matter-of-fact, and unpretty manner, with a slight acerbity directed at our unobservant ways. Observant Ammons, looking under old leaves, and finding life everywhere, exits from the poem "sometimes whistling."

The kind of eye at work in "Bees Stopped," that does not miss the plants growing on rocks, or bees stopping to rub themselves, is also operating in "Butterfly Weed" (a poem of a later period). It watches a butterfly, poised on the weed, flex its wings; the movement is conveyed with fine definition. But for all the alertness of the observer here, a spell is cast on him by the sight; he has become "anchored in / dream," reminding us of the state depicted in "The Grass Miracles."

It is consistent with the poems considered so far that the rural should be wholeheartedly endorsed as the prescription in "Medicine for Tight Spots," offering pastoral release from "big-city / tensions." Working with the fact that "tensions" can refer both to emotional strain and to electricity (as in "high-tension lines"), the poem pictures, in its most memorable phrase, country houses "cool as a single volt." While vigorously asserting the curative effect of bushes and streams, the poem's dimensions are modest, its lines amounting to an advertisement of the country as a nice retreat, one guaranteed to give us balm. The conception here might be said to be that of a city man (which Ammons is not),[1] who feels that "The City Limits," the title of another Ammons work (in which I read "Limits" as a verb as well as a noun). In that poem the city figures only in the title. What lies beyond its boundaries is a radiance that plays over the objects of nature, a radiance that provides Ammons with one of the most intense satisfactions in all of his poetry:

the heart moves roomier, the man stands and looks about, the

leaf does not increase itself above the grass, and the dark
work of the deepest cells is of a tune with May bushes
and fear lit by the breadth of such calmly turns to praise.

This is a much larger and deeper effect than that attempted in "Medicine for Tight Spots."

II   *Nature as Occasion for Stoicism or Melancholy*

Contemplation of nature in Ammons' verse does not inevitably produce feelings of euphoria, whether modest or large. The lighting of "The City Limits," its tone, rhetorical buildup, and overall effect, are distinctly different from the elements of "Way to Go," which defines the world in terms of the natural, but ends only in a sober acceptance. The poem first suggests the haiku, but its last two statements depart sharply from that genre:

> West light flat on trees:
>   bird flying
>   deep out in blue glass:
>   uncertain wind
> stirring the leaves: this is
>   the world we have:
>   take it

As opposed to the exuberance of "Medicine for Tight Spots," or what we might call the implicit ecstasy of "The City Limits," this work is positively tight-lipped. It omits a verb in its first line, and articles in its first four lines. (Those lines can almost be said to exemplify Hollywood Indian English—is Ammons trying to suggest the stoicism we attribute to the Indian?) The poem's beginning indicates an ending, for the flat west light suggests a day's close. There is a flatness in the very manner of the light's stacatto presentation. After its opening line, the poem admits an element of beauty through the presence of the bird, before going on to the wind and its effect upon the leaves. Within its brief space, the piece creates an amalgam of transience, beauty, and uncertainty. Such is the composition of the world we are told to accept. The last line's bare directive, echoing the *t* consonance of the tight-mouthed first line, ends the poem on what strikes me as, at least in part, a grim note.

If the bird in the sky relieves the other elements of the scene in "Way to Go," there are moments in Ammons when the natural provides no comfort, no refuge. These are times when he feels, like Emily Dickinson in "It makes no difference abroad," or Robert Frost in "The Need of Being Versed in Country Things," an unbridgeable gap between the fact of human suffering and the ongoing life of the nonhuman, particularly birds. "Three" contrasts the wholeness of a blackbird's "jeer" with Ammons's sense of brokenness. In "Doubling the Nerve" we are advised that in bleak moments we should "look for no cooperation / from the birds."

Remembrance of other times, other birds, does not help, and the poem stoically accepts the fact of suffering.

In "Sharp Lookout," where Ammons *does* appear to take comfort from nature, that effect is undone. The title here, as so often with Ammons, is in eccentric relationship to the lines that follow, for they unfold in almost a bored manner to assure us about the rationality and stability of the processes and beauties in the natural world. The one deviation from the norm is felicitous: "the clouds that have never taken / shape are shapely." After noting the setting of the sun, Ammons tells us that though he has been expecting some wrenching disruption of the order of things, there is really nothing to worry about. But the nature of his assurance gives us a jolt:

> . . . I've not been able
> today to form evidence of any
> trend countering our prospects
> for a moderate life and a safe death.

The dry, rather weary voice of the poem has produced a last-second shocker. We are supposed to be soothed by the assurance that we will die. Our death is something we can count on, another example of the undisrupted order of the world, as bound to happen as the going down of the sun.

III *Autumn*

Nature provides only cold comfort in "Sharp Lookout." But it can offer even less, becoming itself, as with Dickinson, the locus of disintegration and death (see, for example, "Jersey Cedars"). In this connection it is significant that autumn, its treatment permeated by a sense of mortality, is much more prominent than spring in Ammons' poetry.

"Halfway" pictures birch trees in October, their leaves taken "straight / down" by rain, as standing in

> pools of them-
> selves, the yellow
> fallen
>
> leaves reflecting
> those on
> the tree, that
> mirror the ground.

The beauty of this image softens the stripping of the trees, but at the same time the double mirror effect intensifies the fact of the leaf-fall. The poem's loveliness is compounded of melancholy.

Several poems register the dark encroachment of autumn through viewing the fate of small creatures, such as bees or hornets (see "Equinox," "Lonesome Valley," and "Trouble Making Trouble"). The sympathy of such poems can become empathy as the poet shows anxiety over his own fate. In "The Mark" he hopes that *he* will not be

> . . . right
> where frost
> strikes the
> butterfly:
> in the back
> between
> the wings.

While we might be inclined to see the demise of a butterfly through cold simply as a natural death, the poem makes it seem like a cowardly murder. (The feeling here is similar to that in Dickinson's "Apparently with no surprise," which speaks of a flower being beheaded by the frost.) In "Autumn Song," the poet, on a "brilliant" day, picks up a fallen leaf with an earthworm on it. The worm

> panicked at both ends
> with the threat of drying out:
> a basic
> concern I shared with him
> and share with him

The near cross-rhyme of "panicked" and "basic" emphasizes how fundamental and how shared is the fear. The daylight reveals the worm's arteries, and the poet believes the worm now knows

> he can be seen through and turn
> into a little thong:
> I knew it all along though I'm
> not in grass
> and the leaves that fall
> give me no sense of refuge.

Near cross-rhyme (thong-along) again connects the destinies of worm and man, illuminated by the "brilliant" light of autumn.

Thoughts of the mortality of man and nature are once more occasioned by autumn brilliance in "This Bright Day," where the human and natural fuse in Ammons' poignant consideration of "all that / will pass / away from me that I will pass into." But he claims that while his grief over the dying away of things is as sharp as ever, this feeling now exists in "a higher scale" than it once did, for he now sees a cosmic pattern of destruction and creation in which, interestingly enough, day is associated with the former and night with the latter. He has learned the

> sky, the day sky, the blue
> obliteration of radiance:
> the night sky,
> pregnant, lively,
> tumultuous, vast. . . .

(The "pregnant" night sky looks back to the "huge blackant / - queens bulging / from weatherboarding" mentioned earlier in the poem.) The repetition that makes up the penultimate line of the poem—"space, space—"—and that presumably compresses the day sky and night sky into a unit, suggests the raising of the poet's vision beyond the "Earth, earth!" of the opening line and the original focus on mortality. This might be called the intellectual stance of the poem. But in emotional terms, "space, space—" constitutes a cry, *reinforcing* "Earth, earth!" and leading into the final words of the poem: "a grief of things."

IV   Disjunction between the Human and the Natural

Complementing Ammons' portrayal of the self as intersecting with nature in a shared mortality is his occasional resistance to the notion of the self's capacity to unite with the natural in happier ways. The speaker of "Spring Song," in the very act of scolding rising shoots, apparently for their impermanence, falls in "with their green enhancing tips." He nearly dies in "getting away from the dividing place." This suggests that merging with the tips is a temptation which requires tremendous effort to resist, and that in making the effort the speaker is insisting on the gap between the ultimate needs of the spirit and what nature has to offer. With no

alternative to nature presenting itself in the poem, the speaker
"slaughters" his loyalty. In "Interval," a dream piece (rare in Ammons), the dreamer tells of dropping off to sleep in the woods.
Dreaming of golden feathers falling from a great bird, and of pick-
ing one up, he says "nothing is separable," and points to a pine as
being "almost indistinguishable" from himself. But in a sharp
reversal, he says he does not wish to be a tree "if trees are blind."
Awakening, the golden bird flown, himself in shadow, he moves on.
As with "Spring Song," this poem points to a need of the human
psyche that cannot be met by finding common ground with nature.
(In this connection see "Cascadilla Falls," where Ammons can share
just so much with a stone.) In both works, the integrity of this need
is insisted upon, painful as the separation from the natural proves to
be.

What seems like an echo of a Wordsworthian union with nature
constitutes the starting point for "Gravelly Run," but the poem ultimately comes out in another place. It begins:

> I don't know somehow it seems sufficient
> to see and hear whatever coming and going is,
> losing the self to the victory
>   of stones and trees. . . .

The loss of the self to the stones and trees cannot but remind us of
Wordsworth's "A slumber did my spirit seal," where the "she" of
the poem becomes joined to matter moving in a cosmic pattern:
"Rolled round in earth's diurnal course / With rocks, and stones,
and trees." And even though the opening of Ammons' poem, with
its conversational "I don't know" and its colorless "sufficient,"
seems well removed from the immediate drama of Wordsworth's
poem, "Gravelly Run" moves by a path of its own to something ap-
proaching the Lucy work:

> . . . it is not so much to know the self
> as to know it as it is known
>   by galaxy and cedar cone,
>
> as if birth had never found it
> and death could never end it:

The "as if" keeps the poem's impulse here in check, but the lines
proceed to take on the religious coloring common in celebrations of
nature:

> holly grows on the banks in the woods there,
> and the cedars' gothic-clustered
>   spires could make
> green religion in winter bones:

However, we notice that Ammons is not *in* the woods (which are "there"), and that the verb is in the subjunctive mood. Moreover, the poem goes on to dissolve the unitary effect it had created or suggested. It finds that there is "no / god in the holly," no human philosopher amid the pines. Even the elements of nature, implicitly connected earlier, are seen as separated from each other: "the sunlight has never / heard of trees." Unlike "Spring Song" and "Interval," nature is not rejected here. While wishing to surrender to it, Ammons finds that he is among "unwelcoming forms," and tells himself: "stranger, / hoist your burdens, get on down the road."[2]

The dedicatory poem of *Sphere* has its speaker going into nature and failing to find an image of himself there: "I am / as foreign here as if I had landed, a visitor." He constructs an image of his longing, finds that it completes or fits nothing in nature, and finally brings it back to the city. Nature in this poem will not house or accommodate the human.

V   *Union with Nature*

There are occasions in Ammons' poetry when nature offers or seems to offer the possibility of the self joining with it in happy union (as opposed to union through death or disintegration, the kind we get in "This Bright Day" or some of the earliest poems). "Hymn" pictures the self as entering into the world of nature's minutiae, with the speaker's "ant-soul" traversing a tree's bark (an image similar to one employed in "The Grass Miracles"). The personified loneliness of the camping speaker in "Prospecting" goes out to shake hands with willows and tell "ghost stories to / a night circle of lizards." (This material, uncomfortably close to a cute child's tale, is relieved by the image, Whitmanesque and vigorous, of the loneliness figure as "wet / to the hips with meetings.") After these encounters with nature, the speaker's loneliness awakens him and they go "refreshed" into the day.

Not going so far as a union with the natural, but establishing connections with it, are those poems which locate in nature equivalents or at least metaphors for the human—mind, spirit, and body. In

"Grassy Sound" it occurs to Ammons that "there are no / sharp corners / in the wind / and I was very glad to think / I had so close / a
neighbor / to my thoughts. . . ." While his thoughts in "Corsons
Inlet" originally do exhibit sharp corners ("perpen-
diculars, / straight lines, blocks, boxes"), he is released from these
as his mind comes into correspondence with the events of the beach
setting:

> you can find
> in my sayings
> > swerves of action
> > like the inlet's cutting edge:
> > there are dunes of motion,
> organizations of grass, white sandy paths of remembrance
> in the overall wandering of mirroring mind:

A process very much like that in "Corsons Inlet" is enacted in
"Saliences." The oppressive mental "Consistencies" of that poem
are dissolved by the varying nature of the beach: "multiple as sand,
events of sense / alter old dunes / of mind." "Terrain" defines the
soul, perhaps too insistently, in terms of natural objects or processes.
"Open," a celebration of sex, describes the body mostly in terms of
"canyons, brush hills, pastures." "Viable" links the human and the
natural by comparing the risks the poet takes to the activities of
caterpillars, crickets, earthworms, and redbirds.

Apart from viewing nature in terms that see it as corresponding to
the human, Ammons can make felicitous connections with it,
though without aspiring to grand visions or joinings. "Schooling"
explicitly puts aside those large objects that such visions or joinings
have been grounded on in literature: seas, mountain ranges,
glaciers, rivers, outcroppings of bedrock. It chooses
"lesser / effects," delicate ones, lovingly rendered:

> . . . wind-touch of a birch branch, for
> example, weed-dip, tilting grasses in seed,
>
> the brush of a slipped lap of lakewater
> over a shore stone. . . .

This is nature as Roethke typically gives it to us. We are particularly
reminded of him in the poem's closing words: "be with me wind
bent at leaf / edges, warp me puddle riffle, show me / the total
yielding past shadow and return."

"The Woodsroad" also recalls Roethke. In it Ammons first withdraws from nature and, apparently, from himself. Of the items he specifically relinquishes—clouds, "locust's / burr-squall," "fern's sori" (spore-cases), "caterpillar-pocked / whiteoak leaves"—most are small. If he is giving up the natural he has first been attentive to it. He lets go and floats free. But where in *Ommateum* this might constitute the complete movement of a poem, the transcendence of nature in this later work is no sooner indicated than a reentry takes place, with the self breaking into

> clouds, white dots on
> dead stalks, robin
> mites: then, I'm here:
> I listen: call.

The reassumption of Ammons' human presence in the world has been preceded by his incarnation in natural items—dots, mites—at least as small as those he took leave of. We are in a domain of the minimal comparable to that engaged in Roethke. How humble this fusion with the natural is—the white dots might well be fungoid growths or parasitic insects; parasitic, too, are the robin mites.

The choice of such details gives us the image of the poet as *feeding* on the natural, an image that is, in a way, more striking than the explicit declaration Ammons makes in "Plunder" of the uses he has made of nature, his appropriation of leaves, brooks, "bird music," etc. Though he says at the end of "Plunder" that "my mind's indicted by all I've taken," he has noted that various creatures of nature have also made off with booty. We can conclude that he is no more guilty than they. So Ammons pictures himself here as maintaining ties with the natural, if only by appropriating it for his poetry, without necessarily being gathered into it.

VI   *Imagination's Appropriation of Nature*

Sometimes, even when nature may be conceived of by Ammons as ahuman, indifferent, it can still be put to use by the human imagination, as "Grace Abounding" tells us:

> What is the misery in one that turns one with gladness
> to the hedge strung lucid with ice: is it that one's
> misery, penetrating there as sight, meets neither

> welcome nor reprimand but finds nevertheless a picture
> of itself sympathetic, held as the ice-blurred stems
> increased: ah, what an abundance is in the universe
>
> when one can go for gladness to the indifferent ghastly,
> feel alliances where none may ever take: find one's
> misery made clear, borne, as if also, by a hedge of ice.

What Ammons has done here is to make explicit a strategy employed implicitly in Stevens' "The Snow Man." (Ammons' focus on "misery," a key term in Stevens' poem, as well as his use of "as if," a favorite Stevens phrase, may well be a tipping of the hat to that poet.) "The Snow Man," positing nature as totally separated from human concerns, nevertheless draws on nature to depict the perception of that very separation. Cleaving man from his wintry surroundings at one level, the poem slyly joins the two at another, through its title as well as its crucial phrase "mind of winter." Ammons, possessing the same sense of man's apartness from nature, makes the same sort of joining, but does so openly, and in the process creates a different tone. Nature has been plundered here to give us an unsuffering image of our suffering selves, and its availability for such appropriation is a source of pleasure.

There are other poems where appropriations from nature are made to body forth feelings, but without so unqualifiedly mitigating the emotions they are used to convey. "Windy Trees" and "Pluralist" (the latter possibly owing something to Frost's "Tree at My Window"), draw on natural elements to point up human predicaments, though with wry humor. "Brooks & Other Notions" compares the movements of natural currents and expressions of grief. There is no humor here, no pleasure in the comparison. The tone is somber.

VII   *Questioning of Analogies with Nature*

Not only can Ammons fail to be exhilarated by finding equivalents or analogies for human feeling in nature, he can doubt the validity of looking for such connections in the first place. Such, at least, is my reading of the striking "Reflective":

> I found a
> weed
> that had a

> mirror in it
> and that
> mirror
>
> looked in at
> a mirror
> in
>
> me that
> had a
> weed in it

We have here a sardonic joke. The inverse symmetry of mirror-in-weed and weed-in-mirror parodies the idea of correspondences between man and nature, an idea cherished by Emerson, for example, and, as we have seen, sometimes subscribed to by Ammons. The assumption of such correspondences operates here as a closed system, producing only a fruitless circling. This effect is heightened by the repetition of most of the terminal words: a—a, it—it, that—that, mirror—mirror. Such an arrangement gives us rhyming, or mirroring, with a vengeance. (The typography also produces a repeating effect, through the respective congruences of the two inner stanzas and the two outer ones.) The speaker has garnered no more than the weed he began with.[3]

"Snow Log," a very different kind of poem, also questions perceiving the natural in terms of the human. After assigning intention to the snow, Ammons immediately admits that this attribution of purposefulness is a fallacy. Then, having made anything beyond the given sensory data the construct of the observer, he incorrigibly proceeds to anthropomorphize nature. But he knows just what he is doing.

"Snow Log" ponders nature in a mildly questioning, almost whimsical manner, with an element of depth or behindness in nature only played with as a possibility. But other poems which regard nature as problematical or elusive do so with greater intensity. In "Crevice," after observing that once a mythical conception has been perceived as such the perceiver is cut off from experiencing mythical consciousness, Ammons goes on to say, focusing on a slope, that it retains an impenetrable mystery: "mind can't charge the slope: / again we've fallen wise." I take this last to mean that even the supposedly postmythical mind confronts the inexplicable in nature, and, in so doing, *does* partake of mythical consciousness.

In "Circles," a nature that puzzles is close at hand. The poem
begins with a casual, seemingly supercilious treatment of its
materials:

> I can't decide whether
> the backyard stuff's
> central or irrelevant:

In this phrasing of the alternatives, Ammons seems already to have
come down on the side of "irrelevant"—the backyard growths are
given the back of his hand, not only by being designated as "stuff,"
but by being denied the full copula. However, the poem changes its
manner at once:

> how matted rank the mint is! and
> some of the iris stalks are so
> crooked rich
> the blossoms can't burst
> (scant weeds
> pop their flowers fast) loose
> and the pansies keep
> jointing up another blooming tier:

What was initially "stuff" has now been separated into its parts,
each presented vividly. And as though to compensate for the
originally suppressed "is," the word now makes its appearance
followed by an exclamation point. The scene created by these lines
is one of seething, even oppressive abundance. (It recalls Stevens'
"Banal Sojourn," with its garden described as a "slum of bloom.")
Witness the striking phrase "crooked rich," and the way the placement of the parenthesis, delaying the completion of the thought,
mimics the inhibiting of the iris blossoms. A note of exasperation
may be found in "blooming," which, in addition to its literal meaning, suggests the English slang use of the word as a term of con-
tempt. But the energy of this passage prevents the backyard plants
from being dismissed as simply irrelevant. The poet proceeds to ex-
press his perplexity as he views the explosive growths: "I can't
figure out what / the whole green wish again / is." He cannot sub-
sume the display of vegetative energies under the category of an-
nual patterns or cycles. An immediate urgency is at work, that
"drives in to the next / moment and the next," and he can only
name it the way Frost characteristically names the mysterious in
nature, as "something."

VIII *Instability*

Almost all of "Peracute Lucidity" works, largely through its religious diction, to create an effect seemingly opposite to that of the clotted, confounding activity of "Circles." The poem begins by attributing "A perspicuity like a sanctuary" to its dusk scene. We are inducted with ease, and with a sense of protectedness and perfection, into a pavilion to view the evening. If one of the elements of the scene, "the brookfall's / shaggy seams and rags," makes for a note of disorder or slovenliness, we are restored to elegance by what is above it, "clarity's chapel / bodied by hung-in boughs." Our gaze is carried further upward to contemplate the sky, "blown / cathedral luminous with evening glass." In this setting, the poet experiences a sense of harmony. But the poem's glass cathedral has been constructed only to be broken, for the last words of "Peracute Lucidity" read: ". . . then the stars / come out and question every sound, the brook's." The stars' interrogation creates a fracturing within nature. The last two words, dangling as they do, create an effect of things out of place, in addition to referring us back to the one element of disorder originally in the scene. Beginning with lucidity and a sense of safety, we have ended with questioning and unease.

"Clarity," unlike the similarly named "Peracute Lucidity," seems to live up fully to the promise of its title, although the cause of the rockslide that is its subject remains undetermined—it might have been "rain slippage, / ice crawl, root / explosion or / stream erosive" says the well-informed poet. Nevertheless, the phenomenon itself, which has "realized . . . / . . . grain and fissure," has produced a clear showing forth:

> this
> shambles has
> relieved a bind, a taut of twist,
> revealing streaks &
> scores of knowledge
> now obvious and quiet.

If "relieved" and "revealing" are connected by their shared sounds, there is a possible pun operating in the first term that would further bind the two. In addition to meaning "easing," "relieved" can also be taken to signify "cast into relief," thereby reinforcing "revealing" (thus both words would look back to "realized"). But

even if this is not the case, the poem can be read as implicitly sub-
verting the ostensible effects of easing and quietness that it
associates with clarity. The knowledge given, *now* quiet, has been
brought into being by a radically transforming force that has
produced a "shambles." Part of the clear knowledge of the poem,
then (and in this connection "scores" might well include its use as a
verb, "to cut"), is that of an unstable, potentially violent nature,
capable, through a variety of means, of cracking open the apparently solid earth.[4]

"Impulse," working with a hypothetical situation, rather than the
realized one of "Clarity," provides another instance of instability in
nature. Considering the possibility of a rock on a slope loosening,
the poem asks whether anything will be there to stop it if it does.
The questions making up the poem seem to be put with distinct
anxiety. The rock grows in its threateningness as it requires first *a*
tree or another rock to "be right / there" to stop it, then two of one
or the other. Though not specifically located as to be endangered by
it, the speaker appears frightened by the rock's potential for movement, by the still becoming unstill through a message imparted
from some mysterious source.

"Upland" (like "Impulse" originally published in *Uplands*) ultimately reveals a similar feeling about nature. The poem begins
calmly enough, in a somewhat pedantic manner: "Certain presuppositions are altered / by height." It proceeds to give us vivid examples, then returns to its original stiffness: "a number of other
phenomena might / be summoned." But this display of
detachedness is replaced by something quite different, as the particular instance now summoned is developed:

> take the Alleghenies for example,
> some quality in the air
> of summit stones lying free and loose
> out among the shrub trees: every
>
> exigency seems prepared for that might
> roll, bound, or give flight
> to stone: that is, the stones are
> prepared: they are round and ready.

That which we usually think of as still, is now, as in "Impulse,"
given the potential for movement. The poem deliberately misleads
us in its "every / exigency" statement, making it appear that there

has been a human preparation made against the movement of the stones. But the amplification of the statement assures us only that the *stones* are ready, and the description of them as "round" heightens the sense of their capacity for bounding down. *Our* only preparation is the knowledge, provided by the poem, of a nature capable of surprising us, of altering the presuppositions we may have about the stability of our earth. Looseness, a quality usually savored by Ammons, carries here an implied threat.

All in all, as with most other twentieth-century poets who have dealt with it, nature does not figure for Ammons as it often did in the past: a generalized presence informed by a beneficent or at least significant spiritual force.[5] He concerns himself with particular manifestations of the natural—a bush, a bee, a stone, a tree—and these evoke a considerable range of responses, from theoretical speculation to melancholy, from delight to anxiety. Nature generally does not take him to its bosom (sometimes it functions more like a stepmother) or provide final satisfactions. He can neither house in it nor let it go. It displays clarities yet also raises problems. But revealing or obscure, it continually engages his feelings as well as his mind, vivifying and being vivified by his poetry.

CHAPTER 6

Poetics

A MMONS' critical prose amounts to only a few pages. But again and again his verses take poetry, its characteristics, making or maker, as their subject matter. Poetry ranks with "One: Many" as a principal theme of his, and this chapter will examine those poems which treat of poetry.

For all the frequency of such reflexive gestures, Ammons' poetics is a scrappy one. He has shown little impulse to systematize his thoughts (sometimes derivative), or to make large observations or judgments, except on the fly. Relatively short lyrics, or bits and pieces of longer poems, are apparently considered by him vehicle enough for the great portion of his observations on poetry (which go off in various directions, and are not necessarily consistent). What could be regarded as the one exception to this, the long *Essay on Poetics*, tends to skitter away from its ostensible subject.

I   *Critical Discourse versus Silence*

That Ammons should allow his poetics to be put forth frequently and yet to exist in so sketchy and scattered a state may be seen as a compromise between a compulsion to comment on his art and a conviction that poetry is something best not discussed. The one critical essay he has given us (actually the text of a lecture), takes as its epigraph this statement from Lao Tse: "Nothing that can be said in words is worth saying." Poetry, for Ammons, is obviously an exception to this, but in being so, makes the statement applicable to itself. A poem, he says, "becomes, like reality, an existence about which nothing that can be said in words is worth saying."[1] Transcending logic, a poem is itself impervious to logical analysis. It incorporates so complicated a process of awakening and directing energy that "you cannot say anything clear about it except about a small part of it."[2] Such statements appear to make "the heresy of paraphrase" a trivial stricture, virtually replacing it with a notion of the heresy of discourse.

The ineffability that applies to the individual work extends to the whole genre. Such is the consequence of Ammons' adoption of the organic theory of form (undoubtedly taken from Coleridge and Emerson—Ammons is in the peculiar position of ostensibly eschewing poetics even while subscribing to well-known critical ideas, besides putting forth some of his own). "Each poem," he says, "in becoming generates the laws by which it is generated: extensions of the laws to other poems never completely take." This is an example of the "logically insoluble problem of one and many." Complete consistency with his obscurantist stance would require that he be virtually silent on the subject of "poetry." As a matter of fact, he says in "A Poem is a Walk" that on that subject "silence is finally the only perfect statement."[3] But he has not been able to maintain it.[4]

A critic only in spite of himself, Ammons is drawn to silence even in his poetry. I noted, in Chapter 2, the celebrations of silence to be found in *Ommateum*, where it is connected to the eternal, with the embrace of it being a corollary of the desire to leave the world behind. In *Expressions of Sea Level*, both in the title poem and in "River," silence, associated with the changeless or ultimate, again exerts an attraction. A poem of *Corsons Inlet*, "Configurations" (to be discussed more fully later), presents silence in a way that suggests its superiority to speech. *Tape* considers the possibility of giving up words and "coming home . . . / into silence" (*T*, 87). Like Mallarmé's celebration of the virginal whiteness of the page, such a prizing of silence (not uncommon in contemporary poetry), might well put an end to the making of poems. Ammons, of course, has not permitted this to happen to him.

But he has made silence an element of his poetics. In *Essay on Poetics* he says, in effect, that he can have poetry and silence together. The progression of a poem, he states there, "is from sound and motion to silence and / rest" (p. 310). He made a similar point in an interview. As a poem completes itself, he asserted, one is "left in a state of silence. You now know where all the motions are. . . . The motions are all reconciled when motion ends."[5] This statement may help explain the opening line—"From silence to silence"—of "Breaks" (examined earlier), a work which centers on his poetic act of speech. The first silence is that of the world, a given unity, which Ammons breaks by his utterance. The second silence is the ultimate effect that his words produce, through reconciling the multiple motions that they initially generated.

Fracturing the original silence in "Breaks" is accomplished by a speech that Ammons claims "declar[es] the cosmos." This is perhaps qualified by the description of that speech as "skinny"; nevertheless, declaring the cosmos certainly seems a grand enterprise, if a vague one. Grand and vague too is *Tape*'s declaration that poetry "realizes reality's potentials" (*T*, 177 - 78). Such context as the poem supplies for this remark is not especially helpful. For in the vicinity of this statement *Tape* stresses the need for "cool control" in poetry, then shifts to a call for *power*. Realizing reality's potentials first seems to be a matter of refining emotion, then of intensifying it.

II   *Poetry and One: Many*

Ammons claims for poetry (and this is of obvious importance to him) the capacity to reconcile the One and the Many (see *Essay on Poetics*, p. 315). In fact he has said that such reconciliation is possible for him only in poetry, which he characterizes as "the fuzzy land of radiant talk" (*Hibernaculum*, p. 369). The near-oxymoron here (something like Stevens' "ghostlier demarcations, keener sounds"), is itself a kind of reconciliation. If "fuzzy" suggests something dubious about the poet's enterprise, Ammons does not seem exercised over the matter, the tone of the passage in question being relaxed and humorous.

Poetry's ability to reconcile the One and the Many is closely related in his mind to Coleridge's statement in *Biographia Literaria* that the power of the poet's imagination "reveals itself in the balance or reconciliation of opposite or discordant qualities: of sameness with difference; of the general, with the concrete; the idea, with the image; the individual, with the representative; the sense of novelty and freshness, with old and familiar objects; a more than usual state of emotion, with more than usual order. . . ." Ammons, joining a large chorus of celebrants, has said in "A Poem Is a Walk" that this passage constitutes the "greatest statement in our language" about poetry.

III   *Limits of Poetry*

Coleridge's statement imputes great power to poetry. Ammons is apparently happy to subscribe to such a view, but is not always able to do so, stressing instead the limits of poetry, or at least his own. "Mountain Liar" is a humorous example of this. The aged speaker, no Orpheus, keeping "no lyre," agrees to help the mountains get off the ground. With poet and mountains closing their eyes, the whole range flies, or believes it does. When this proves to be an illusion, the lyreless poet emerges as a liar (bringing to our minds Plato's accusation). He cannot transform reality but only create momentary illusions. In "Alternatives" Ammons wistfully calls for an Archimedean lever with which to move the world. He once believed he could do it with words, but realizes that this was only a dream.

If the poem is limited in what it can do with or for the world, it is limited in what it can do for the poet as well. "Medium," employing a Christian vocabulary (uncharacteristic for Ammons), reserves the grace that comes to the poet for the poem alone. He himself is an unredeemed medium.[6] The title, together with the stanzaic arrangement (the poem shifts from one stanza form to another at its midway point), serves to effect a separation between the poet and his poem. Whatever the virtues of the latter, the former is morally unchanged.

But while "Medium," in its humility, severs the poet from his creation, affording him no moral comfort, "Triphammer Bridge" conceives of the poem, at least by implication, as something that gives shelter to the poet:

> . . . if I
> think the bitterest thing I can think of that seems like
> reality, slickened back, hard, shocked by rip-high wind:
>
> *sanctuary, sanctuary,* I say it over and over and the
> word's sound is the one place to dwell: that's it, just
> the sound, and the imagination of the sound—a place.

Word has displaced world here, the mind and ear becoming their own place, a refuge from bitter reality. The power of language and, by extension, poetry has been affirmed.[7]

IV   *"Configurations"*

A sense of poetry's power exists in tension with a sense of its limitations in the complex and troubled poem "Configurations," cited earlier. This is one of Ammons' most remarkable works, although it has received little or no attention. Stevens' "Thirteen Ways of Looking at a Blackbird" probably served as one of its models. It recalls that poem by its division into numbered sections (fourteen to Stevens' thirteen) which are self-contained, epigrammatic (at least for the first six sections), conscious of mortality, linked (though not as completely as in Stevens) by a bird or birds, and concerned, at least in part, with poetry.[8] On the other hand, Ammons' poem allows itself typographical arrangements (one meaning of the title) and certain liberties of a kind not found in Stevens' works. Also, the parts of "Configurations" are less disjunct than those of "Thirteen Ways"; while Ammons' poem has its gaps, they occur principally in the form of sharp shifts of view and tone.

"Configurations" takes an empty nest as the starting point for its meditations. (In the context of Collected Poems, this emptiness functions with particular force, since the two pieces preceding "Configurations" feature singing birds.) Stripped by November, the shrub in which the nest is located hangs in "essential limbs." Seen in conjunction with the poem's fourth section, which speaks of a secret working itself into life when the shrub was "shadeful," the "essential" can be identified as the fact of death. This is the secret originally concealed by summer's foliage.

Bareness, coldness, dryness are the principal effects created by the poem's first four sections. Their somberness is not relieved by the appearance of speech in the fifth, for this is described as "a bleached form, / nest-like," not much of a recommendation, particularly when we remember that the original nest was empty. Moreover, Ammons goes on to suggest that speech is a fall from "the events of silence."

Minimal as it is, the nest, in section 6, serves as analogue for the intelligence. Just as the nest is held off the earth by sticks, so intelligence is "erect on a / brittle walk of bones." This in itself is not very reassuring, but the alternative to such precarious separation of mind from earth is "the sea, / empty of separations." Thus, no great claims for speech or intelligence have been put forth so far, but, the poem may be implying, they are all we have. In section 7, "Configurations" again focuses on death, linking, as it had before, leaves to wings, and wondering if "dry wings / lie abandoned."

With section 8, the poem effects a kind of quantum jump, a leap into play and humor:

> I am a bush
> I am a nest

        I am a bird
        I am a wind
        I am a negg

        I is a bush, nest, bird, wind, negg
        I is a leaf

We not only have a sharp change of tone in these lines, but the new
and prominent appearance of an I, that is, Ammons (he had been
absent in the first six sections, and suppressed, through blatant
omission of the first person pronoun, in the seventh). His holiday
with speech does not sustain the poet, and his playful equations are
replaced by a thought which makes him part of an ongoing pattern
of mortality, operating without end: "if I fall what falls: / the leaves
fell and the birds flew away and winter came and."

But in section 9, the power of speech, or rather poetry, is asserted
in the face of disappearances:

        when
        I
        am   bringing
        singing those   home
        ,   two   again
        summer birds
        comes
        back

The power of the poet to restore the birds, to break free of a
seemingly inevitable pattern, is given formal embodiment in his
free use of typography to produce this unusual specimen of the
shaped (wing-shaped?) stanza, a pattern of his own exuberant
choosing. His power over language creates a reality, in the form of a
verbal configuration, to replace that which has been lost (notice the
singing-bringing rhyme—the second word brings back the first, so
to speak).

Buoyed up by his sense of power, Ammons, in section 10, dismisses other possible consolations for the loss of things, placing
supreme value on the shape he can make, though that shape now
figures as a mental configuration. But even as he does so, the shape
dissolves, apparently pulled into the pattern that he had earlier
defied. Permanence now becomes associated not with anything of
his own making, but with "proximity / to the earth." Yet when, in
section 11, the poem's objects—earth, shrub, nest, leaf, bird—are

arranged in a column apparently according to this criterion, even the shrub is shown to be vulnerable, included in the series of good-byes that concludes this section.

In section 12 the poem replaces its preceding farewells to what presumably are actual objects (regarded as either individual or typical) with the assertion that those objects exist only as elements of the poem:

> the shrub is nothing
>   except part of my song:
> the bird I never saw is part of my song and
>   nothing else:
>
> (the leaves are a great many little notes I lost
>   when I was trying to make the song
>   that became my silence)[9]

Having, through this statement, divested itself of everything except a self-referential content, the poem, in another switch, once more focuses on a pattern that seems to exist outside itself, a chain of endless desire (though that desire seems to modulate into the force of gravity):

> the cockbird longs for the henbird
> which longs for the nest
>   which longs for the shrub which
> longs for the earth
> which longs for the sun which longs for

The ongoing pattern at the end here recalls the final line of section 8: "the leaves fell and the birds flew away and winter came and."

"Configurations" concludes with a section in which the life-force that wishes to restore the lost leaves is dampened. The "woodmeat" pleads to put on its leaves, but the "zero bark" says "it's not the right time / the woodmeat is always right / but bark is knowing."

While, as I have indicated, there is a formal resemblance between "Configurations" and Stevens' "Thirteen Ways of Looking at a Blackbird," I would like to suggest that we can best gain a perspective on Ammons' poem as a whole if we see it as being in ironic relationship to Shelley's "Ode to the West Wind." That work, like "Configurations," has an autumnal setting, and is permeated with the consciousness of mortality, dramatized through fallen leaves (together with clouds and ocean). As Ammons does with the objects of his poem, so Shelley links himself with those of the "Ode." Shelley does so less radically and abruptly than Ammons, but more seriously. Where Shelley exclaims "Oh lift me as a wave, a leaf, a cloud," Ammons says, with conscious excess and humor (parodying Shelley?), "I am a bush / I am a nest / I am a bird / I am a wind / I am a negg." Shelley enjoins the West Wind to be his spirit, to be him. The concluding lines of his poem suggest that his imperious prayer will be answered, while in the case of Ammons the flat statement "I am a wind" (particularly notable since this is the wind's first appearance in the poem) is followed by the pratfall of "I am a negg" (this is the egg's first appearance as well). Shelley's poem moves sweepingly, in unbroken *terza rima*, from his original consciousness of death and disease to a sense of reborn energies, an unquestioning confidence in his poetic powers. After the sustained somberness of its early sections, Ammons' poem oscillates, in constantly varying stanzaic form, between two contrasting moods: a bravado based on his power to create patterns and on his identifying poetry with reality, and a despair proceeding from his consciousness of inexorable patterns outside his poetry that govern existence. Where Shelley concludes with "If Winter comes, can Spring be far behind?" Ammons may be said to end with the thought that if Winter comes, Spring will have to take its time about returning. Leaves serve both poets as symbols of their own words, but those in Shelley are going to "quicken a new birth," while in Ammons, rebirth is impeded by the "zero bark," his wintry consciousness. In *Tape*, Ammons declares that "Poetry has / one subject, impermanence, / which it presents / with as much permanence as / possible" (*T*, 145). If hardly true of all poetry, the first part of this statement certainly applies to "Configurations." That poem, while making large claims for the power of poetry, is troubled by a sense of the forces or patterns that cannot be coerced or transcended by the poet.

V *Poetry and Reality*

"Apologia pro Vita Sua," an earlier work than "Configurations," showed the confidence of the latter, rather than its doubts, conceiving of poetry as a monument standing in opposition to or defiance of reality. The speaker here erects a pile of stones, which rises above the surrounding slate and sand. This cairn is designated, in the poem's last line, as "a foreign thing desertless in origin." Set off by its height, its alien quality regarded as desirable, the cairn is the speaker's apologia, and calls to mind Stevens' "Anecdote of the Jar," with its celebration of artifact over nature.

But the sharp distinction between the two in "Apologia" has not proved characteristic of Ammons' sensibility. Even while insisting on the distance between reality and language, hence poetry, Ammons is anxious to keep them connected. He says in *Essay on Poetics* that while language is removed from reality, it must not violate the factual and concrete, otherwise it will die (p. 298). "Spiel" tells us that the mind's freedom is not absolute but dependent on fact: "fact / is the port of / extreme navigation," the last phrase apparently signifying far-reaching excursions of the imagination. The concept of creating a world in poetry radically distinct from what exists is given short shrift in "High Surreal":

> Spit the pit in the pit
> I told the cherry eater
> and see what crumbling
> shoulders, gully washes,
> & several other bardic
> dimensions can produce:
> possibly a shiny asbestos
> tree with cherry
> nuts—reversal obvious
> in the formation—but
> if you come to impossible
> productions on
> absent trees, get out the
> bulldozer and shove the
> whole thing over smooth.

Plunging from the ostensible height of the title to the depth of the mischievously gross first line (expectoration made verse), the poem instructs poets not to seek that which violates nature but that which enacts it. The "bardic / dimensions," we see, are simply earth's phenomena, destructive and creative at once.

Here, Ammons is offering advice on what seems to be a matter of choice, but in *Hibernaculum* he sees the poet as dependent on reality, in a particular sense, whether he likes it or not. That poem scoffs at the notion of the autonomy of the mind, and is content to believe that "mind and / nature grew out of a common node and so must

obey common / motions" (p. 358). The natural restrictions on
mind, Ammons says, actually "release me into motion" (p. 359). Existing structures take care of the functioning of much of our world
and our selves, thereby giving us freedom to create or contemplate.
Such a view does not make for a romantic or symbolist elevation of
the creative imagination, but for a humble gratitude toward what is,
the imagination's sustaining context.

VI *Poet and Society*

Several of Ammons' poems address themselves to the question of
the status of the poet in relation to his society. "Conserving the
Magnitude of Uselessness" works its way to this matter after first
regarding certain natural elements which, of little or no practical
value, obviously interest Ammons. These range from "Spits of
glitter in lowgrade ore" (a phrase which mines them for the ear) to
things sublimely useless:

> the peerlessly unsettled seas that shape the continents,
> . . . the gales wasting and in waste over
> Antarctica and the sundry high shoals of ice. . . .

The poem itself is an example of its defiant contention that poets
celebrate the useless, the "worthless," and the "unimprovable."
Slyly waiting almost to the end of the piece to make his point, Ammons indicates that poets have been relegated to just such
categories—they are "rank as weeds themselves and just as abandoned." (The comparison to weeds takes on special weight when we
remember Ammons' predilection for those growths, for example in
"High and Low," commonly regarded as worthless.) In a similar
spirit, he observes in *Tape* that poets are free to do and say what
they like since nobody will react much one way or the other (*T*,
182). (On the other hand, the early "I Assume the World Is Curious
About Me" sees the poet not as ignored, but crucified.)

However, Ammons' works do not inevitably assume the stance of
the poet alienated from an indifferent society. He seems intent, in a
number of places, on building bridges between the poet and other
men. In "The Watch" he portrays himself as a watchman, ready to
warn the rest of us of impending danger. "Poetics," seeing the poet
as a kind of conduit rather than autonomous creator, speaks of
shapes that want to be realized "through me / from the self not

mine but ours." The poem, ending here, does not spell out this self, but the point is that Ammons sees it as collective, a property held in common with other men.

Even the assertion of the "uselessness" of poetry can be found apart from an alienated posture. In his lecture "A Poem is a Walk," after characterizing walks and poems as useless, Ammons does not leave the matter there but formulates a social function for art: "Having once experienced the mystery, plenitude, contradiction, and composure of a work of art, we afterwards have a built-in resistance to the slogans and propaganda of over-simplification that have often contributed to the destruction of human life."[10]

Essay on Poetics puts forth another social use for poetry, in attributing to it the power of reconciling the One and the Many. The poem is seen as "the symbolical representation of the ideal organization." It shows how the One and Many can cooperate, how organizations can incorporate change, thereby "assuring the probability of survival" (p. 315).

VII *Poetry and Pain*

Whatever social benefits may accrue from the *reading* of poems, the *writing* of them is often regarded by Ammons as coming at great expense for the poet. "I Struck a Diminished Seventh" shows the poet-speaker functioning as a unifier, or would-be unifier. Awaiting "the universal word" that will bind earth and air, he fails to receive it and is dissolved by death. This radical ending, while clearly characteristic of *Ommateum*, in which "I Struck" originally appeared, also serves to adumbrate works of later books. Notice, for instance, "Spindle," a poem that appeared in *Corsons Inlet*. There, song is characterized as a "violence" that makes "an organized whirl" out of heterogeneous objects, "relating scrap / to scrap in a round / fury." Thus song, or poetry, is again conceived of as bringing diverse, discrete materials into relationship, into a whole. But what I wish to emphasize is that the poem, giving a last-line fillip to this notion (and breaking the three-line stanza form it has employed), describes song as "a / violence to make / that can destroy." Perhaps what is destroyed is the integrity of the original, separate materials (the Many sacrificed to the One) or the intended form of the poem. But the words can easily be taken as designating the poet himself.

Certainly, the intense, portentous diction of "Spindle" is just one instance of a strain that runs through a good number of Ammons' poems, insofar as they concern the poet's act of composing. The making of a poem is repeatedly treated as a painful, involuntary servitude (this is the dark side of Ammons' notion of the poet functioning as a medium). "Joshua Tree" depicts the poet as lonely, anguished, wandering through desert country, enslaved by his vocation, suffering some blockage, some impeded birth of language, from which he can only hope to be released. *Tape* describes the Muse as a woman "who sets / fire to us, gives us no / rest / till her / will's done" (*T*, 2). Ammons asks of this taskmistress "will you tear me / to pieces?" (*T*, 45). The priestess at the god's oracle in "The Strait," who should be taken, I believe, as representative of the poet, is described as writhing and moaning, caught up in anguish, "seized / by her struggling / mouth into / a speech of / forms." Near the end of the piece, she is "god-torn, limp." The protagonist of "He Held Radical Light" experiences the transformation of "his head to music." When this happens he is thrust to height, and seeks to escape from the "high . . . hook." Seen against the background of these passages, "Laser," which presents an image as seizing the mind, may be regarded as another example of the painful coercion of the poet's psyche.

All this material adds up to a portrait of inspiration akin to the notion of the poet in Plato's *Ion* as possessed by a divine power.[11] Without necessarily regarding inspiration as coming from a divine source, poets have repeatedly offered testimony to the *involuntary* nature of their composition, and, as Stanley Burnshaw has pointed out, aesthetic theory has often excluded volition from the creative process.[12] But the association of such involuntariness with outright pain has generally not been as insisted upon as it is in Ammons, though Eliot, for example, has spoken of writing poetry in order "to gain relief from acute discomfort."[13] Burnshaw, seeing the composing of poetry as the result of a disruption in the cycles of accumulation and release characteristic of the human organism, notes that such disruption "manifests itself in a variety of states, from vague excitement or tension and irritability to malaise, severe discomfort, even pain."[14] What figures as an extreme in this formulation is regarded as typical by Ammons.

If the poet's productions have sometimes been explained as the result of some seizure from outside himself, they have also been regarded as deriving from internal, personal pressures. Ammons has expressed this view as well. On the first page of *Tape* he juxtaposes "Inspiration" and "Unconscious," and later, he speaks of the "volcano-mind" emitting a "ribbon of speech, / smoke & heat / that held / would bust the cone off" (*T*, 13). (This volcano imagery may owe something to Byron's "the lava of imagination whose eruption prevents an earthquake.") In *Extremes and Moderations*, after speaking of the explosive potential of "the cumulative vent of our primal energies," Ammons refers to that poem's open stanza form as "my ventilator" (pp. 340 - 41).

Powerful and painful feelings are seen as the generating force behind verse in "Composing." This poem, employing a number of musical metaphors, views the act of artistic creation as an "orchestration" of "wounds," among other things. There is "an emergence / of minor meanings, / . . . the critical cymbal / crashing grief out." The term "minor" can be taken in its musical sense, minor keys often being associated with the mournful. The grief can be interpreted either as having been expressed or gotten rid of—the two meanings of course are complementary. As the poem proceeds it speaks of the "dark resurrections" of "mangled" ghosts. But these are put to rest with the completion of artistic creation. Here, as in *Tape*, poetry is regarded as a way of coping with painful memories that, unless expressed, might overwhelm the psyche. The title "Composing," then, in addition to serving as a musical metaphor designating the making of a poem, also works to suggest the purpose of that making, namely, the poet's reaching for a state of release or rest, of *composure*. (The poem so uses its participial phrases as to keep itself up in the air, so to speak, until its last four lines allow it to complete itself, to come to a semantic rest.) "Muse" also employs musical terms and regards the poet's making as coming out of pain.

In a few instances in Ammons, pain is not necessarily confined to his personal experiencing of it, but is something which he confronts in his capacity as a visionary. That is, it exists as something outside as well as inside himself. An example of this can be found in "Doxology." *Essay on Poetics* speaks of how "the / orders of the poem build up and cooperate into the pure heat of / sight and insight, trembling and terror" (p. 312). In *Pray Without Ceasing*, poetry's confrontation of the world's pain is central. That poem, like "Path," seems to fuse Ammons' own pain with a vision of suffering external to him.

VIII   *Poetry and Pleasure*

Despite all the evidence that the Muse and pain are inseparable for Ammons, there is a considerable discrepancy between his so joining them and the actual spirit of much of his verse, which has generous amounts of contentment, joy, and delight. If he did not repeatedly insist on linking poetry and pain, we could not, in reading many of his works, have deduced for ourselves that the two for him are so closely connected. Moreover, there are a number of places in his poetry where he explicitly gives us the figure of the poet as being someone other than a man mournful and racked. While these instances may involve serious and even painful materials, they are strongly suffused with wit, humor, and gaiety. For example, in "Return," a poem concerned with the drying up of poetic powers, Ammons is able to imagine himself in ridiculous postures. "Positions," which considers his poetic reputation (or lack of it), says that "everybody who is neglecting me . . . / . . . is incurring a guilt complex / he'll have to reckon with later on / and suffer over." "Reassessing," which follows immediately on "Positions" in *Collected Poems* (the two are part of a series of six, all stating Ammons' needs), refers to the making of verse as a "lowgrade hallucination" (this wittily suggests "lowgrade infection"). It further describes his vocation as "primitive tribal hooting / into some wooden or ratty totemic ear," which is certainly a funny version of the unappreciated poet. In "Up" Ammons presents himself as a blustering clown. If there is a suggestion that he may have the clown's proverbial hidden sadness, the main effect of the poem is one of exuberance and self-delight. "Precursors," which appears to be an allegory about Ammons' awakened sense of literary predecessors, employs "puddles" to designate various poetic domains as well as his own (while this is a far cry from the "realms of gold" and "wide expanse" employed by Keats, the poem is not denigrating poetry, for the puddles serve as a source of wonders). The use of the puddles metaphor to begin with, as well as the terms "dibbled" and "scribblings," gives the poem a quality that keeps it far removed from associating the making of verse with pain. Ammons' own puddle is referred to as a "dawdling hole,"[15] and "Precursors" invests the making of poetry with something of childlike pleasure, discovery and play.

"Spiel" presents the poet as a spieler, that is, a voluble talker, confronting an obscure, discontinuous reality whose phenomena, both large and small, claim his attention. The term "spiel" also means "to play," and that is what the poem does. Considering a spider's possible source of nutrition, Ammons says

> droplets
> drift dripping proteins loose that
> drunk skirl spiders into hallelujahs
> of darkening:

This is virtuoso play with sounds, resulting in a comic magnification of the micro-materials. The poem regards reality's plenitude as close to overwhelming, a too-muchness which is relieved by existing forms. The poet adds his forms, forms of play. (A poem on the page following "Spiel" in *Collected Poems* is entitled "Play.") But the poet's verbal forms and games can only struggle with reality, not master it. This, at any rate, is my interpretation of the poem's closing lines:

> sporting goods
>
> nip and tuck
>
> scoops
> scopes
> scrimps &
> scroungings

The poet's enterprise is a series of improvisational games or spiels, but these, attempting depth (scoops) and range (scopes), are ultimately meager (scrimps & scroungings). The lines are making a serious observation, but their language delights in itself in the very act of pointing to the limitations of language. One is reminded of Stevens' "Children of poverty, natives of malheur, / The gaiety of language is our seigneur," though in the case of Ammons, we should replace "poverty" with "overabundance."

The image of the poet as a spieler, a talker or player, strikes me as a paradigm more suitable for Ammons than the image of the poet as seized by the Muse, or as pain-wracked and seeking composure. The two different conceptions come together in *Essay on Poetics*, where Ammons, after talking of the "trembling and terror" a poem builds up to, relates poetry to "fun," and says "poems are pure joy, however divisionally they sway with grief" (p. 313). This last statement, along with other materials we have been looking at, rightly modifies the portentous, solemn conception of the poet and his poetry that Ammons has put forth a number of times without qualification.

IX *Poetry and Motion*

When Ammons focuses on poems per se, he frequently sees them as words in *movement*. Motion and meaningful use of language are inseparable for him. In *Essay on Poetics* he says "the verbal moves / . . . or sinks into unfocused reality" (p. 310). Any word is always poised over the pit of meaninglessness: "stop on any word and language gives way" ([p. 298]—and remember that in the first poem of *Collected Poems* the name "Ezra" is reiterated, and Ezra dissolves, "As a word too much repeated / falls out of being").[16] Ammons' observation about language giving way may be referring to the common experience of having a word turn into nonsense through repeated utterance or through being contemplated in isolation, but apart from this he could be focusing on the necessity of motion in language because of motion's importance for him as a characteristic of reality. While it may be essential for language to be "artificial," removed from reality, it must simultaneously be connected to reality, and *is* so connected through its motion. The music of poems, Ammons says, "by the motion of / its motion / resembles / what, moving, is—." (This statement occurs in a poem fittingly titled "Motion.") "Viable" makes a similar point: "sound and motion" are the symptoms of life, with "the poet, too, moving and / saying. . . ." In his comparison of a poem to a walk, Ammons points to motion as the feature common to both. Even when, in *Essay on Poetics*, he speaks of the silence and rest toward which a poem's sound and motion moves, he qualifies this by adding that "when the mind is brought to silence, the / nonverbal, and the still, it's whole again to see how motion goes" (p. 310). That is, from the still point achieved, it is the poem's *motion* that is contemplated. This idea distinctly qualifies Ammons' contention, quoted earlier, that in a poem "The motions are all reconciled when motion ends." Ammons' reaching for a still point from which to look at motion is analogous to Yeats' conceiving of the golden birds of Byzantium being removed from time and change, yet taking those as the subject of their song. Neither poet can rest in stillness the way Eliot does.

Ammons' preoccupation with the motion of a poem may help explain his predilection for the colon, the ubiquitous presence of which has become a trademark of his verse. (*Sphere*, a work of over 1800 lines, uses commas and colons exclusively, consenting to employ a period only at its conclusion; *Tape*, over 200 pages long, does not have a period at all.) His use of the colon may be seen as a reluctant acknowledgment of the necessity for marking semantic pauses in his verse (in the poems of *Ommateum* there was no punctuation whatsoever, with the exception of "Doxology"). But even as it creates a pause, the colon also sustains movement, imparting a thrust forward, because its presence suggests that what follows it will be necessary for the completion of what has come before.

Ammons' "A Note on Prosody," a prose piece analyzing some lines of his own, again focuses on motion, treating what he sees as his poem's *downward* movement in terms of a waterfall.[17] The handling of poetry in terms of water imagery occurs repeatedly in Ammons. This may derive in part from the traditional association of water and fertility or fruitfulness. For the poet, of course, such fruitfulness would take the form of his capacity for utterance. (See "Joshua Tree," "I Struck a Diminished Seventh," and *Tape* [*T*, 1].)

But apart from the traditional linking of water and fertility or creativity, Ammons' joining of the two derives largely, I believe, from his thinking of water as being in flow or motion. *Essay on Poetics* arranges the orders of increasing greatness in poetry in terms of different forms of water, going from drops, to brooks, to a river, to the ocean. Motion is explicitly ascribed to the last three forms of water, and is incipient in the first (since the drops are produced by a "snowline melt" [p. 309]). *Tape* makes several connections between poetic creativity and fluid in motion.

Ammons sometimes presents his water-motion-poetry complex in images of power, as in "Corsons Inlet," *Tape* (*T*, 179) and "Spiel." In "The Limit," one of Ammons' most extensive figurings of verse as water in motion, he is uncertain about the extent of this power, but plainly attracted to it. After calling the left-hand margin of this (or any) poem "the clear edge of imposition," Ammons says

>   . . . the other the
> thrusting and breaking to possibility:
> in between
> a tumbling, folding under,
> amounting to downward
> progression:

the prisoner is not much enamored of compression:
I wonder if this slight
tumbling, brookish, is a large enough motion
to prevent lodged sticks & harrow beavers:
apparently it
can
reach out broadly across the page in space-hurry gesture:
the events a stick makes
coming down a
brook
scraping the bottom
of the ledge-smooth spill. . . .

Here the comparison of the movement of verse to that of water is combined with Ammons' notion that the direction of such movement, at least in his works, is *down* the page (though the longest line in the passage is about reaching out *across* the page, itself enacting that "space-hungry gesture"). The event-making stick that comes down the brook may be punningly referring to a composing stick, which prints a line of type. The "events" made by this stick, or more correctly, a collection of these sticks, would include, among other things, the continually changing line lengths of a poem such as this. For despite its title, "The Limit," the poem's heart is not with the limit of the unchanging left-hand margin, but with the freedom of the continually shifting margin on the right. As the poem itself says, it "is not much enamored of compression." Perhaps there is a kind of irony in having the last word of this statement rhyme with "progression." The rhyme only accentuates the radically different lengths of the two lines involved, and in so doing, may be intended to remind us how far the free verse of this poem is from poetry employing the restriction of the couplet form, where the rhyming and equal length of two successive lines is, of course, the norm. In short, the poem is more concerned with progression, with the power of its motion, than it is with compression, or limits.

To shift terms slightly, "The Limit" prefers *flow* to *shape*. There is a dialectic of the two running through Ammons' poetry. In "Muse" he prays to be made "into a changed brilliant shape." "Poetics" has him looking for forms, "being available / to any shape that may be / summoning itself / through me. . . ." The titles of these two works suggest that the arrival at shape is central to the making of poems. At the same time, "The Swan Ritual," which is about the composing of a poem, presents the poet as first entangling or trapping himself in the poem, then as breaking out "beyond all binds and terminals." This pulls against a stress on shape.[18] Also, as has been indicated, Ammons' use of water imagery shows that verse is associated in his mind with flow.

Can shape and flow be integrated? In "Countering" Ammons envisions having both of them. He speaks of the "crystal of reason" growing down into his emotions, "casting me to / shine or break." The "brilliant shape" of "Muse" is recalled by "crystal" and "shine," though now there is something undesirable or dangerous ("break") as well as attractive about such a shape. "Countering" concludes by talking of retaining both "life and/ shape." To do this Ammons says he hides

> contours,
> progressions between
>
> turning lines,
> toward the higher
> reason
> that contains the war
> of shape and loss
> at rest.

The notion that he somehow conceals both shape ("contours") and flow ("progressions"—see "The Limit"), so as to keep them, is confusing, as is the war metaphor. Is he saying that he hides these elements as they operate in the individual lines of a poem in order to retain them for the whole? The passage strikes me as vague and merely wistful in its assumption of some sort of synthesis.

At the beginning of *Extremes and Moderations*, Ammons appears to be suggesting that he can achieve such synthesis without too much trouble:

> constructing the stanza is not in my case exceedingly
> difficult, variably invariable, permitting maximum change
> within maximum stability, the flow-breaking four-liner, lattice
>
> of the satisfactory fall, grid seepage, currents distracted
> to side flow, multiple laterals that at some extreme spill
> a shelf, ease back, hit the jolt of the central impulse: the
> slow working-down of careful investigation, the run
>
> diffused, swamped into variable action. . . . (p. 329)

The stanza he is referring to is the four-line stanza used almost throughout the entire poem. It is said to break the flow, but it does not do a very thorough job of this. Consider the metaphors: the form makes for a "side flow," it allows "seepage," the "satisfactory fall" (which can be taken as the enjambment of the stanzas—the "fall" has been enacted just before being named), as well as the "spill" of one line to the next ("spill," like "fall," is aptly situated). The downward run of the verse may be "diffused" and "swamped," but notice how the latter verb operates. For an instant it seems to be supplementing "diffused," and to mean "made into a swamp," suggesting stagnation rather than movement. But as the line continues, the verb produces the opposite effect, that of activation. Though the passage may speak of "maximum stability," the emphasis is on flow.

Near the close of *Extremes and Moderations*, the lattice image is used again, with no suggestion of a synthesis of shape and flow, but with stress on the second: "my lattice work . . . lets the world / breeze unobstructed through" (p. 341). Shape here has been discarded or at least subordinated (and the poem goes on to refer to itself as "a flatness . . . without beginning, / development, or end"). But even in the original use of the lattice, shape figures only in a limited, mechanical way. The poem has "shape" in the sense of possessing uniform typographical units for most of its length, but the question of shape in the larger sense of overall design or coherence has not been engaged here.

Nevertheless, the poet's act of shaping is celebrated in *Hibernaculum*, through a spider image:

> . . . the heroic
>
> entangler, benign arachnid, casting threads to catch,
> hang and snatch, draw up the filamental clutch, the
> clump-core reticulate, to tie energy into verbal knots
>
> so that only with the death of language dies the energy!
> so all the unravellers may feed! . . . .
> . . . . . , ... pleasure to my tribe and
>
> sufficient honor! . . . (p. 356)

Despite this praise of knotting or shaping (a kind of aural knotting takes place through the cross and internal rhyming of catch—

snatch—clutch), the poet's enterprise is later questioned in language that recalls this passage. We are told that the poet "entangles," hopes to arrive at "*the* core-tangle that will / fix reality in staid complication" (p. 372, italics in original). Ammons says of this "what an / illusion," a comment which undoubtedly stems, at least in part, from a deep distrust of fixedness, stoppage of flow. That flow may be the streaming of physical events or of consciousness. In either case Ammons wants to honor it in his poems.

"If Anything Will Level with You Water Will" appears to be a clear exception to this, but ultimately is not. It moves from regarding the fluidity of water to contemplating and celebrating the solidification of rock, which it conceives of as petrified water—"a bound slurp." The rock, once molten, has cooled "to exact concentration." Here, surely, is arrested flow. But we should note that the rock is "old material." It can be placed at one end of a scale, on which the other items are "old streams from which the water's / vanished," streams having lithified sediment, and "modern streams," in that order. The scale, then, goes from solidity to liquidity, and from ancient to modern. This arrangement appears to be the vehicle for a symbolic statement about poetry. Ammons admires the "old material," old poetry, which need not be "read" (I think this means "interpreted" or "deciphered") because "it says itself." That seems to constitute the ideal for him. But he, after all, lives beside "modern streams." These "drop loose composed figurations. . . ." He must, by implication, construct shapes that are loose, that do not readily say themselves, shapes that make for flow. It is such forms that are the subject of the next chapter.

CHAPTER 7

Linear Modes

THE early poem "Choice" describes a mysterious struggle with a god who "rolls up circles of our linear / sight in crippling disciplines / tighter than any climb." Whatever meaning the poem originally had for Ammons, I would suggest that it takes on a particular significance as we look at it from this point in his career, which has seen the production of several long poems. The "crippling disciplines" can be interpreted as those he has submitted to in composing works that are relatively short and coherent. In writing these pieces he has had to deny a natural, if not invariable, tendency to *expatiate* (in the verbal equivalent of its original sense, "to walk about at large, to roam without restraint"), to move in a line from one subject to another; instead, he has had to make a given work curve back on itself, assuming a shapeliness and interlocking of parts.

The poems so achieved he seems to see as limited. *Essay on Poetics*, a long poem, speaks of the lyric in terms of a *bending* of materials into a curve, "one curve, the whole curve," resulting in a "wholeness" (p. 296); while not explicitly used, the figure of the circle, I believe, is clearly suggested here. But this curved wholeness is seen to have been achieved at the cost of scope. Later in *Essay* the lyric is referred to as a "slight completion" (p. 298). It is opposed, as such, to what Ammons calls "a linear mode," examples of which are dactyllic hexameter and blank verse. One infers that Ammons does not mean so much to designate specific meters here (it makes little sense to compare a kind of poem to a particular meter) as to suggest the large forms in which those meters have been used, namely, classical epic and some of the more formidable works of English literature. That such is the case is indicated when he says dactyllic hexameter "can grind on, entangling, ingesting bits, / threads, strings, lesser saliences into considerable scope," and when he calls iambic pentameter, "especially unrhymed, . . . an infinitely

111

various / ployable means" (pp. 298 - 99). "Linear mode," then, seems to be a shorthand notation for a large form, one that can attain scope, that can, in its digesting of diverse materials, register the multifold nature of reality. "Linear" indicates that its thrust is forward, the extension of a line, so to speak, rather than the forming of a circle.

This mode moves from point to point, giving primacy to that which enters its immediate view, rather than looking over its shoulder so as to relate its incoming parts to those which have preceded them. What it loses in shapeliness and immediate coherence it gains in inclusiveness and variety. As with the burgeoning backyard of "Circles," so with the linear mode: "something nearer than / the pleasure of / circles drives into the next / moment and the next." Constraint oppresses Ammons. He is drawn to what he calls "Ramshackles, archipelagoes, loose constellations" (though the clicking consonance of this line, which opens "The Unifying Principle," holds it together even as it opts for looseness—Ammons is no advocate of pure chaos). His mind ranges widely and he likes to give it rein, to allow it "swerves of action" and the flow he so prizes. This he does primarily in his long poems. These works, repeatedly raided for illustrations in my earlier chapters, need to be considered in themselves, as individual entities. They are the subject of the present chapter.

I   Tape for the Turn of the Year

While awaiting the appearance of *Expressions of Sea Level*, Ammons labored, from early December, 1963, to early January, 1964, at completely filling an adding machine tape with

> a long
> thin
> poem (*T*, 1)

The typography here humorously points up his intention, but the enterprise (which recalls Jack Kerouac's method of writing) was for the most part a serious one. The resulting *Tape for the Turn of the Year* is Ammons' single longest work so far.

On reading the first page of the poem, one is struck by the doubleness of Ammons' conception. Announcing his intention of writing a long poem "employing certain / classical considerations," he initially seems to be carrying out a mere exertion of will,[1] inviting us to witness a *tour de force* of composition based on the arduous recipe for an epic. In keeping with this, he tells us that "first the / Muse / must be acknowledged, / saluted, and implored." But no sooner has he given us the impression of some mechanical exercise being carried out, than Ammons lets us know the genuineness of his invocation to the Muse. She is not for him an archaic literary convention, but, however designated, a real force. The poet, then, who first seemed to be strutting forth on the strength of his will, reveals a deep sense of dependence on something outside that will.

Invoking the Muse repeatedly, Ammons addresses *Tape's* most passionate lines to her, lines employing sexual imagery;[2] thus, as in other of his poems, he joins sexual energy and poetic creativity. There is at least one sharp departure from this treatment of poetic inspiration in a passage that might almost have come from the Psalms or George Herbert or Edward Taylor. But here too Ammons posits his dependence on a superhuman force outside himself, on the "Lord" (*T*, 141).

Considerably less exalted is *Tape's* dependence on what the daily round of the poet's life turns up. For in embarking on his long, thin poem, Ammons seems to have no *a priori* subject. He is simply allowing the blankness of the tape to be filled with whatever his immediate future will bring. He says at the end of the poem that he wrote about the days "the way life gave them: / I didn't know / beforehand what I / wd write" (*T*, 203). *Tape*, then, while partly an exercise of will, is also an extended experiment in poetic passivity, and one that brings to mind the prose forms of diary and journal.

Nothing, of course, could be further from epic, which the poem's opening lines have, in effect, evoked. Ammons explicitly recognizes this gap, saying "I wish I had a great / story to tell," then distinguishing between himself and Odysseus (*T*, 8 - 9; see also 29). At the same time he indicates he does have a story to tell, claiming "it is / in a way / a great story," dealing with "how / a man comes home / from haunted / lands and transformations" (*T*, 9). We hear almost nothing more of this for almost two hundred pages, so that if the poem *is* possessed of a story, it is well concealed. What Ammons may have had in mind is the distance he has traveled between *Ommateum* (1955) and *Tape*. The former may be said to construct a series of haunted lands and transformations (through transcendence or dissolution), while the latter steeps itself in dailiness, the mundane. But *Tape* does not record a journey from one to the other; it is "home" from the start.

Expressions of Sea Level had done much to get Ammons there, but mainly by endowing him with a past. *Corsons Inlet*, published in the same year as *Tape*, was largely impersonal, or else employed stylized situations and speakers (including Ezra) reminiscent of *Ommateum*. Its opening poem, "Visit," at first apparently functioning like Frost's homey invitation to the reader in "The Pasture," ended by presenting the poet as a kind of hermit naturalist, welcoming us, but on his terms, his sociability qualified by his requiring "a dense reserve / of silence" (p. 130). *Tape*, however, works to give us the poet as a man much like other men, not primarily, as in *Expressions*, through memories (though these are present, overlapping with those in *Expressions*), but through his immersion in ordinary circumstance. We become acquainted with a poet who lives in a house, has a wife, operates a car, listens to the news, observes the weather (rather too much!), eats franks and beans, recounts jokes, performs Christmas chores, urinates, goes to church (in this respect, *Tape* is like "Christmas Eve"). Though composing verse on an adding-maching tape is hardly an ordinary occupation, it functions in the poem as that which most other people have to face, a daily task.

But while Ammons uses the poem to establish his kinship with common situations and doings, and while the notations of these serve to fill much of his long, thin *tabula rasa*, he does not hold back from pursuing those concerns that mark his particular and very special sensibility. So we see him meditating on form and motion (or flow), on order and energy, center and periphery, oneness and multiplicity. For him the daily is intersected by his considerations of these and of the underlying physical laws that sustain ordinary existence. He is especially impressed by and grateful for the complex mechanisms of things, including those of his body, which, operating automatically, make possible the free exercise of consciousness.

It could be that his appreciation of the sustaining mechanisms of existence, together with his sense of a reality too complex for understanding, helps account for *Tape's* quietism, optimism, conservatism, and piety. Discontent may flicker, but is not allowed to dominate. For example, in considering disease and death, Ammons moves from "bitterness" to acceptance (*T*, 60). He may refer to unmentionable memories "of guilt & terror!" but he removes their sting by not specifying them, and by enjoining us to "take it on / faith" that "we knew no better" and are now repentant (*T*, 136 - 37). Later in the poem he wonders if he has "glossed over the / unmistakable evils" (*T*, 153); he eventually says "we must bear / the dark edges of / our awareness" (*T*, 155). The term "edges" is fitting because darkness is generally kept at the margins of consciousness in the poem; there is not much bearing Ammons asks us or himself to do, and he goes on to say that "beside the terror-ridden / homeless man / wandering through / a universe of horror," there lives "the man at ease / in a universe / of light." God has brought us this far and "millions have come / & gone in joy / (predominantly)" (*T*, 155). In thus subordinating the homeless man moving through horrors, *Tape* is drawing away from a characteristic preoccupation of twentieth-century literature, and one reflected in *Ommateum*. But the propensity to fall into alienation is challenged here only by a glib affirmation. Such affirmation also appears in Ammons' view that the direction of history is that of increasing unity and peacefulness on earth—as evidenced by the United Nations! (He does acknowledge that there has been much slaughter along the way.)

When *Tape* considers the human potentialities for delivering hurt, the allegorical figures through which it represents them are caricatures, and even this thin rendering of evil is dissipated (*T*, 186 - 87). Inasmuch as Ammons admits he is "afraid to visit" the domain of destructive passion, he cannot expect us to accept his optimism. It is a view through a distancing lens, an Emersonian concentration on long-range tendencies rather than local textures, the sort of vision that Ammons would question in "Mean" (see Chapter 4, p. 58). The poem's optimism would seem to make it easy for Ammons to "come home," a movement he equates, near *Tape's* end, with both "self-acceptance" and "going along with this / world as it is" (*T*, 203).

This, I find, is the dominant stance of *Tape*, but the work is not without some tensions and doubts, though these are centered more on the making of the poem than on the world. At one point, Ammons stands back from his words to say "fact is, I'm having / this conversation with a / piece of paper!" (*T*, 46). His self-appointed task of filling the tape seems to him an "obsession, senseless, / slightly mad" (*T*, 49). (Earlier, he punningly refers to the "story" his poem is telling as growing like a "tapeworm" [p. 10]). He questions his "need to throw / this structure [the poem] / against the flow" he cannot stop, that is, the passing of the days (*T*, 87). Why should the reader, he wonders, abandon "the running honey" of his own, actual life to come to the poem (*T*, 88). Why should Ammons himself? He confesses to the notion of putting words aside in favor of "immediate / deed" (*T*, 89; see Yeats' "Words"). Regarding himself as removed from ordinary reality by poetry, he enjoins himself to "merge with coming & / going common life: / drink / the average / drink" (*T*, 181). Paradoxically, not only does Ammons' concern with flow move him to question his art in *Tape*, but so does his attraction to shape. He fears that through his poeticizing he is "probably / converting the fine, / shaped, / differentiated world / into / undifferentiated grist" (*T*, 102). "[L]eave structure / to the Maker," he says, "& praise / by functioning" (*T*, 142 - 43).

But of course these are not *Tape's* only sentiments on the matter. If they were, Ammons could hardly have gotten through his roll. Even when he calls himself, as poet, "a fool who / plays with fool things," he tells us he wants to make fools and their play "rise in the regard of / the people" (*T*, 2). His own, Sisyphean labor of writing *Tape* may strike him as a little mad, but his fine retelling of the story of Sisyphus (*T*, 76 - 78) can be taken as a celebration of the poet's work. Poetry "needs no / appeals beyond itself" (*T*, 50). Although the writing of it may sometimes seem to remove him from reality, the terms he uses in *Tape* to describe that writing approach or fuse with the very metaphors of "flow" by which reality is designated (see *T*, 65, 73, 101). This indicates how much, for Ammons, life *is* the act of composing verse, riding the stream of one's works. (What I have taken as an address to the Muse in *Tape* [*T*, 192 - 94] can also be read as an address to reality.)

Nevertheless, Ammons does fret in *Tape* about his removal from living, his isolation, his conversing with paper. Perhaps as a relief from such feelings, he repeatedly and explicitly directs his attention to the reader of the poem. Though at the time of composition that figure could only have been a shadowy one, the assumption of his existence probably helped relieve Ammons of his doubts, providing him with a justification for his strenuous task beyond that of the poem for the poem's sake. So if Ammons, in *Tape*, is socializing himself by setting his slightly nutty labor in an extensive context of the ordinary, he is also socializing himself by openly reaching out to the reader, partly as *semblable*, but distinctly not as *hypocrite lecteur*.

While he may tell us that he and we can "exchange / gaps" (*T*,

196), he also comes to us as the strong man uplifting the weak. Like
Whitman, who says to the reader of *Song of Myself,* "You
there, / impotent, loose in the knees, / Open your scarf'd chops till
I blow grit within you," Ammons says to his reader, named as a
"clod," that he will show him to be "unlike a
clod: . . . / . . . oh, burn, / transfigured sod! (*T*, 190 - 91). He
commands us to dance, to throw ourselves "into the river / of
going: / where the banks also flow" (*T*, 191). In this passage Ammons may be said to arrive at a resolution of the conflict between
his desire to leave poetry so as to immerse himself in life, and his
wish to continue in the service of the Muse. The flow of his words is
directed here to urging his readers to plunge into the flow of existence. Poetic vocation joins up with life through the audience.

But even after this passage, Ammons' consciousness of the reader
can take the form of apologizing for his poem. He claims to have
"bludgeoned" us "with every form of / emptiness" (*T*, 195). This is
one of several instances in *Tape* (see *T*, 5, 144, 153, 204) where Ammons appears to be anticipating charges that might be leveled
against the poem by making them himself. Such a procedure strikes
me as having something of the calculating and self-protective about
it, though it could be the expression of a real humility. At any rate,
this approach does not dispose of those charges.

Ammons seems particularly concerned about his poem's exhibition of "emptiness" or "blankness" (see *T*, 195, 204), and in this he
is rightly worried, for *Tape* contains a good many blank verses. In
giving his poem up to the "days / the way life gave them," Ammons inevitably committed himself to recording trivia, and to marking time when the flow of consciousness ran thin. Certainly, the
Muse deserted him during his ruminations on social order and social
restraints (see *T*, 107 - 9 in particular), and on the state of the world.
These are not his proper subjects, as the following lines
demonstrate:

> this ole world could be
>   one
>   if it wusn't
>   for hate
>   bustin it apart. . . . (*T*, 89 - 90)

What is this but platitude in pop lyrics? As the passage continues, it
speaks of love rising up and of "children" dancing, "shaking breasts

& hips, / pelvis / shooting in & out" (*T*, 90). Such an image of utopia seems drawn from American Bandstand, a television dance show directed at teenagers.

In effect, Ammons defends the blank or dull passages of *Tape* in three ways. First, speaking to the Muse about "bringing this / stuff up," that is, the poem's varied materials, he says he may thereby be cleansed (*T*, 127). But even if the filling of the tape any which way could achieve this worthy end, why conduct his aesthetic purging in public? (He even seems to doubt a little later in the poem [*T*, 136] that such purging will occur.) Another defense appears on *Tape*'s penultimate page, which splits up into two lines of argument. One is that the poet has decided to show himself as he really is, not living at a constant pitch of inspiration and creativity, but "sometimes / blank & abstract," and all too human in his failings. The second line is that the poem is like life itself, "bending, / weaving, changing, / adapting, failing, / succeeding" (*T*, 204). But surely these are egregious examples of the imitative fallacy. To depict Ammons' blankness, did *Tape* have to go blank? To point to the flow of existence, did the poem have to put itself completely at the mercy of that flow?

If Ammons originally conceived of his poem in the terms just examined, he was surely right to wonder why the reader should turn aside from his own life to peruse it. But he must have had higher hopes for his work, or at least some notion of a long form that would not require defense or apology. He says, less than a quarter of the way through the poem, that life without structure is meaningless and that he will make a "trellis so / lovely & complicated that / every kind of variety will / find a place in it or on / it" (*T*, 44 - 45). A related passage tells us that he has been looking for

>   . . . a level
>   of language
>   that could take in all
>   kinds of matter
> & move easily with
>   light or heavy burden:
>   a level
>   that could,
> without fracturing, rise
>   & fall
>   with conception &
>   intensity:

> not be completely
> outfaced
> by the prosaic
> & not be inadequate
> to the surges. . . . (*T*, 143 - 44)

Such a quest is ambitious and commendable, and *Tape*, by being in turn diarylike, speculative, anecdotal, didactic, and reminiscent, and by incorporating a considerable variety of subject matter, gives evidence that Ammons hoped to fulfill his quest for a flexible, omnivorous verbal instrument within *its* pages.

But contrary to such a hope, *Tape*, in rising and falling, *does* fracture at a number of points. Some of these breakages are purely linguistic, involving a sudden, distinct shift in diction. In several places, Ammons switches, to no apparent purpose, from standard English to dialect (see *T*, 33); and, in another kind of switch, he writes lines that are made to sound Elizabethan (*T*, 68 - 69). Elsewhere, a rainy day is described in Germanicized English (*T*, 189). This excursion into a Sid Caesar routine is fun, but sticks out as a very light comic exercise, serving to point up the verbal doodling Ammons must use from time to time to feed the empty tape.

Another kind of fracturing occurs through sharp changes in focus or tone, and one suspects that Ammons has effected these in a deliberate, self-deflating way, as though afraid to appear pretentious in what he has said just before the point of breakage. For example, in wondering if he can ever complete the filling of the tape, he asks "will the Muse fill it / up immediately and let me / loose? can my back / muscles last?" (*T*, 3) The jump from an elevated notion to a mundane physical consideration can also be found when Ammons, just after telling us that art tries to achieve "timelessness held / at the peak of time," reports that he "went to take a leak" (*T*, 38). This may well have been the case, but recording it seems designed not so much to present the unvarnished truth as to puncture what has just been said. As a final example, consider what Ammons gives us after one of his poem's longest meditations, a passage of sustained seriousness which has endeavored to strengthen our spirits, and urged us to join the dance of life: "and when / you can / get laid / get laid" (*T*, 125). One can only say that this is tasteless. In all these instances Ammons has not had the courage to put forth his feelings or beliefs and let them go at that. He seems compelled to assume the role of entertainer, forcing his poem into self-destructive pratfalls. Or perhaps these tonal breaks I have been noting are formal manifestations of his discomfort over being removed, as a poet, from ordinary life, with the sharp descents in language and tone meant to show the poet as a regular feller.

Tape claims to have its own "kind of veracity" (*T*, 143). Perhaps Ammons locates this in the poem's exhibiting the vagaries of the poet's creative enterprise, his having to contend with the blockages of the flow he wants to ride, his being subjected to the in-and-out pattern of energies in the workings of the world. (Such energies are repeatedly referred to in the poem.) In any event, *Tape* may be said to have its own kind of daring in presenting its maker as it does. Its way is not really that of confessional poetry, which, in featuring the poet's terrors, sufferings, angers, or humiliations, confers on him the interesting intensity of his exacerbations. Ammons has risked giving us an image of himself immersed in doldrums and dailiness. He can show that dailiness as touched with the wondrous, but frequently it is for him merely what it is for the rest of us. Indeed, the poem is too often subdued to what it works in, and by its own criterion—"only the lively use of language lives" (*T*, 176)—fails us repeatedly. Its riches—such as its description of a stripped Christmas tree (*T*, 151 - 53) and of a hawk ascending with its prey (*T*, 191)—are thinly scattered through its two hundred and five pages.

II   Essay on Poetics

If *Tape*, in part, attempts to justify its composition by regarding itself as a necessary prelude to "short rich hard / lyrics" (*T*, 143), *Essay on Poetics*, originally published in 1970, after Ammons had written a number of such poems in the interim, offers no comparable self-apology. Moreover, its opening stanzas, appearing to build to a sense of climax and accomplishment, do so only to create an anticlimax through which *Essay* conveys its belief in the limits of lyric poems. As indicated early in this chapter, *Essay* claims that while the lyric can produce a sense of wholeness or completeness, it is a minor form, possessed of limited scope.

In place of the lyric, *Essay* advocates a kind of poem that furnishes a sense of rich process rather than neat conclusion (see p. 300). The lyric offers a single center, but "reality is abob with centers: indeed, there is / nothing but centers" (p. 299). If I read *Essay* correctly, it does not dispense with the notion of arriving at a center, but it desires one that conveys a sense of the multiplicity of reality. We are, then, confronting the familiar issue of the One and the Many, the poem itself declaring that that is what it "is about" (p. 300).

If the poem's title has led the reader to believe that the work is going to be about principles of poetry, or only about such matters, he is quickly, joltingly disabused. The opening is an impersonal, rather abstract and forbidding affair, heavily dependent on Ammonisms—"periphery," "salience," "one-many," "scope." But at least it is about lyric poetry. However, with the last stanza of the first page, the poem abandons its opening mode to give us an *I* discoursing in a relaxed and accessible way—about cowpaths! (On a second reading of *Essay,* one can detect Ammons jokingly adumbrating this leap by using "beefing up" as a metaphor in his treatment of the lyric.) The paths in question are not so much the actual things as imagined aerial photographs of them, on the basis of which our poet can make deductions and a prediction. From recording of data (or at least hypothetical data) to induction to prediction—Ammons has enacted in miniature a demonstration of scientific method. Moreover, the poem as a whole is as striking an illustration as one could want of Ammons' predilection for scientific matters and musings (in its last four pages, *Essay* quotes extensively from scientific texts). So much for the work being merely about poetics.

After the digression on cows, Ammons appears, for a moment, to be herding himself back into line, using an extended cow metaphor to characterize "loose speech," that which he has just presumably indulged in. But he does this only to declare that he does not care about his poem wandering off, since "there's no market for most speech, specially / good, and none for loose" (p. 297).

Still, for all its waywardness, *Essay's* subject matter falls within a few main categories: One and Many (or relatedness and diversity), physical and biological phenomena, poetry. Moreover, while *Essay* may *jump* from one of these subjects to another, sometimes within a single stanza, the poem can be regarded as reaching for an integration of Ammons' characteristic preoccupations. It considers biological structures or mechanisms as examples of diverse entities or processes coming to a kind of unity, and its treats a poem as effecting a unification of its diverse materials. Both the human organism and a poem are examples of *organization* (a recurring term in the work),[3] reconciliations of the One and the Many, and *Essay* links them directly (p. 312). In so doing it may be said to bring its own seemingly disparate materials into relatedness or unity.

But while *Essay* professes to believe in the reconciliation of the One and the Many and attempts the integration of its own variety of subjects, it sets up resistance toward such reconciliation and integration. Moreover, the poem shows a general tendency to be skeptical about its formulations and conclusions. For example, at one point, having said "the problem is scientific—how is reality to be / rendered," Ammons goes on to note "I / have the shaky feeling I've just said something I don't trust" (p. 310). After developing an elaborate series of metaphors in which different forms of water are made to represent different kinds of poetry, he anticipates our reaction this way: "but will you say, what of the content—why they are all made of water" (p. 309). This is a joke—but on whom? Very possibly, not just on the reader but also on the poet, who may fear that he has been carried away by his analogies. Furthermore, he realizes that he may be hoisted on his own petard, that is, be subjected himself to another, unflattering water analogy, involving "mist or vapor" (p. 309). (This kind of explicit self-doubting is more attractive than *Tape*'s implicit self-undermining.)

If Ammons cannot always rest easily in his own statements on poetry, neither can he accept unqualifiedly the assertions of others. He points up the inadequacy of William Carlos Williams' famous prescription for the poet, "no ideas but in things." Ammons finds that there are alternatives to this: " 'no things but in ideas,' / 'no ideas but in ideas,' and 'no things but in things' " (p. 308). Ammons is suggesting that Williams' formula is not the only desirable procedure open to the poet (Ammons himself often follows the alternative "no things but in ideas," using objects to attain a high degree of abstraction). When *Essay* considers another well-known formulation about poetry, "the transcendental / vegetative analogy," meaning, presumably, the kind of comparison between a poem and a tree, say, bequeathed to us by Coleridge and the German romantics, Ammons says he would like to go along with this; yet his knowledge of how a tree actually operates, namely, that its growth pattern is not purely spontaneous but largely dictated by the genetic code built into it, causes him to find the idea of "organic becoming . . . / . . . only partially / adequate" (p. 316).

Further consideration of the matter takes him away from his original emphasis on organization and from the confident statements he had made about the beneficial effects of reading poetry, to contemplation of the chancy, open, and dangerous. *Essay* now notes the limits of the artist's consciousness and, in effect, questions his autonomy, showing him as limited both by *a priori* conditions and by unpredictable, uncontrollable happenings. There is a humility in these musings (p. 316), a humility which can also be found in Ammons' giving *Essay* over, on its concluding page, to a quotation from *Scientific American* about the life of an estuary, which is at once rich and precarious, subject to catastrophe. Through the use of the quotation, Ammons may be suggesting that the enterprise of the poet is also rich and precarious. It works with a medium, language, which must be removed from reality but not too far removed (p. 298), which strives for clear denotation but evokes, willy-nilly, the connotative (p. 301), which has to avoid both artificial clarity and dizzying complexity (pp. 301 - 2), which must flow but whose springs in the poet may dry up (p. 313).

Essay on Poetics, as already indicated, does not proceed in systematic fashion, focusing exclusively on its declared subject. It swerves and meanders, its changes of focus working against its prosy nature. That is, while its verbal texture is largely that of expository prose, it does not unfold with the orderliness of such prose. As a matter of fact it humorously denigrates orderliness: "(disquisition is sesquipedalian pedestrianism, tidying up / the loose bits, but altogether missing the import of the impetus) . . ." (p. 299). There is an obvious playfulness in the language here, but such playfulness is not characteristic of the poem. *Essay*'s animus against disquisition is manifested less in a play of language than in a play of mind, in idiosyncratic jumps, that turn out to be less wayward than they first appear. Fascinated both by the multiplicity of things and by the organization he finds in or among them, Ammons is trying to get the diversity of his own sensibility into the poem and at the same time organize it. In so doing, he roots poetry in a world whose complexity is both entrancing and humbling.

III   Summer Session

Summer Session (named for a college term often devoted to classes for visiting students) and *Pray Without Ceasing* are among Ammons' most interesting poems. Approximately of the same size, they are shorter than *Essay on Poetics*, but each is, I think, harder to grasp. *Essay* does offer difficulties because of its variety and its occasional abrupt jumps from one subject to another. (Also, it carries a relatively heavy load of ideas.) At the same time it possesses a recurring concern with poetics, and throughout its diversity it steadily *discourses*. It may shift focus suddenly, but it maintains (with some exceptions) a relatively even tone, that of a thoughtful, if digressionary, lecturer. This evenness is heightened by the poem's use of a particular form—long-lined tercets—for most of its pages.[4] *Summer Session* and *Pray Without Ceasing* are much more erratic affairs, not only in their shifts of subject and scope but in their changes of tone (which extend over a considerable range) and in their continuous use of irregular stanzas or line lengths. They are much more expressive poems than *Essay*, giving vent to intense emotions, and much showier in their use of language. They take pleasure in that use, and contain elements of humor, but also display some very dark moods. Both, in effect, announce themselves as poems of a man in his forties[5] (as such they can be compared with Stevens "Le Monocle de Mon Oncle"). Two of Ammons' most fragmented and most troubled works, they might well be considered as companion pieces. Each (particularly *Pray Without Ceasing*) challenges the reader to discover ways of bringing its separate parts into relationship.

In drawing on the daily circumstances of Ammons' life during a particular period, *Summer Session* is similar to *Tape*. It displays Ammons directly, as a husband and father as well as a teacher of poetry-writing courses. But the poem is not confined to such a presentation; rather, again like *Tape*, it interlaces the circumstances of the poet's everyday life with observations of natural phenomena and with free-ranging meditations.

Beginning on a note of gaiety, *Summer Session* proceeds to talk of the setting out of tomato plants, whose progress the poet wishes to examine:

> but coming dark hinders me,
> forcing faith up which
> must
> spindly as high walloping
> weeds
> outlast the night. . . . (p. 248)

The vocabulary of this evokes a religious ordeal, spirit being tested by a dark time, but it does so comically, the "walloping weeds" overshadowing, by forceful sound and nonsense content, any serious suggestion of spiritual trial.

The poem's initial mood has not, then, been broken, and is

further sustained in the next, short stanza. But the following stanza
is another matter. It first gives us a humorous depiction of "yurp-
ing" dogs coming to assail the poet as he walks home from class. His
response is fanciful, but the fancy just barely contains his very real
anger: he hopes that worms will close off the dogs' eyelids "the
way / summer closed up the / hedges to fill / us with surprises" (p.
248). The anger not only breaks sharply with the original mood of
the poem, but gives us an unsettling view of the poem's season,
relating it to an act of blinding and dubious surprises.

Some spelling out of the contents of the season is given in the
next stanza:

> in my yard's more wordage than I
> can read:
> the jaybird gives a shit:
> the earthworm hoe-split bleeds
> against a damp black clump. . . . (p. 248)

Even in its few details, the stanza well illustrates it opening statement. Ammons appears to be saying that he cannot bring the
natural functioning of the bird and the cutting of the worm into a
coherent configuration. Certainly, the respective ways in which
they are presented are sharply different. The bird's single line
moves quickly, coasting on its vulgarism. Only after we have
uttered it might we pause to notice how Ammons has humorously
restored the phrase to its literal meaning. But the two lines given to
the worm, stressful and implicitly distressed, admit of neither speed
nor humor. What, Ammons may be asking, does this backyard
tableau add up to? If he cannot read the wordage here, he has in
some sense been blinded by summer.

The poem now poses another problem, undergoing another disjunction. For the next stanza, consisting of the statement "the
problem is / how / to keep shape and flow," does not seem to link
up with bird and worm, but to put in general terms the problem of
retaining in some sense the precious shapes of nature, which would
mean, in effect, freezing time, while still maintaining the flow of existence, also precious.[6] The putting of the question initiates a series
of meditative stanzas which first focus inward, setting the passing
away of things against the power of memory, then turning outward
to the ongoing shapes of nature, seen as consumers and destroyers,
themselves subject to breakdown. But while mortal, they provide

for their reproduction, holding "figuration in the cast seed" (p. 249). Nature, at least, seems to have solved the problem of keeping both shape and flow.

Ammons follows this observation by saying "we must not feel hostile" (p. 249). The context indicates that he is referring to the order of things in which we all die. The poem continues for several stanzas to assent to the order of things, the order of motion, examples of which include the rotation of the earth. Dropping from this to a tongue-twister and sports trivia, Ammons then embarks on a new movement and mood, revealing troubled feelings rather than the preceding acceptance of the *status quo:*

> past 21
> women suffer
> unbearably (!)
> take bladder irritation: that headachy
> backachy feeling:
> that burning stitching itching gives them
> the weewee's, making them need
> fast relaxing comfort: what women go
> through
> to make or lose a buck: in those
> ample haunches
> greased with sheer illumination's light
> is a mess of bacterial bloomers: it's
> merciful to lust the eye's
> small-blind: cultures from average nipples:
> knowledge is lovely
> but some of it shivers
> into the blood stream
> and undermines the
> requirements of the moment: but
> desire spills antiseptic gold celluloid
> sheathes o'erall
> and pours pellucid lubricants
> down the drains of microfloral
> habitations. . . . (pp. 252-53)

What starts out here as a solemn statement is, after an ambiguous exclamation point, quickly subverted by the entrance of advertising language and the undignified "weewee's." But this joking about female troubles is supplanted by what appears to be a serious and uncomfortable view of certain facts about women's bodies. The diction in which this is registered makes for a distinctly unstable amalgam. It moves from the qualifiedly tributary "ample haunches / greased," to the elevated, honorific "sheer illumination's light," to the colloquial, pejorative "a mess of" and the punning "bloomers." Here the data of biology is uncharacteristically found repellent by Ammons, giving us woman as germ-carrier. As it proceeds, the passage attempts to get past this revulsion, but fails, with its terms getting in each other's way. The assertion that "desire spills antiseptic gold celluloid / sheathes o'erall" is strained, both in its peculiar image of sheathes being spilled and in its poeticism of "o'erall." "Sheathes" is supposed to designate an insulating of the self from the knowledge that shivers it, but the term undeniably conjures up condoms, which are supposed to prevent spills. (Was Ammons thinking of the other function of condoms, which once had to be merchandised as "solely for protection from disease"?) Moreover, if we look at what "pours" and at its destination, we get the peculiar compound of "pellucid lubricants," and the near duplication of the colloquial expression "down the drain," meaning "lost" or "wasted." "Microfloral," taken by itself, is a relatively attractive term, apparently working against "down the drains," but it acquires a negative charge when we realize that it is simply a prettier version of "bacterial bloomers." All in all, the passage seems close to the anguished definition of lust in Shakespeare's Sonnet 129 ("An expense of spirit in a waste of shame").

While a poem that comes out of a very different feeling about sex, Marvell's "To His Coy Mistress," appears to shadow some of the lines in the next stanza of *Summer Session,* those lines mainly pick up Marvell's sardonic words about the prying worms in the tomb, and not the charm or passion of his poem. Ammons reports having told his wife that worms will "scoff" at them.

> what are
> a few vaginal weeds in the teeth
> compared with the traipsing gluebellies of
> candorous maggots: & other worms,
> all their noise:
> get down, yes:
> enwarm to eradication the carnal
> longings: which are short. . . . (pp. 253-54)

There is a deliberate grossness here, unrelieved by the wit present in Marvell's equivalent lines (". . . worms shall try / That long-preserved virginity, / And your quaint honor turn to dust, / And into ashes all my lust"). Also, Ammons' invitation to sex comes first as monosyllabic and minimal ("get down") and then as stuffy and abstract ("enwarm," etc.). This is a far cry from the combination of the concrete and the grand in the powerful concluding section of Marvell's poem. The treatment of sex here is particularly striking, because Ammons usually presents it with humor or delight, or else associates it with poetic creativity. A related association is now given to us in the next stanza of *Summer Session*, but it operates to denigrate the two things associated, the poem claiming, with some punning, that the soul's high moments are, like orgasm, brief. For something over a page, then, *Summer Session* has displayed a mood markedly dour and disturbed.

At this point, we get a distinct shift of feeling, effectuated by something that could only occur in Ammons, the consideration of a procedure for observing ducks defecating, the scientific question being "do / they do do underwater" (p. 254). Having delivered himself of this comic formulation, based on a child's term for excrement, Ammons jumps to a sophisticated level of language for an alternate designation of the duck's feces; in performing his observation, he says, he would "count the dropping abstractions off" (p. 254).[7]

Scientific objectivity, which "puts / radiance on / duckshit even," has combined with linguistic play to produce a passage of high spirits. The humor comes from a nicely manipulated diction, as opposed to the mixed terms of the "bacterial bloomers" passage, where the troubled feelings seem to generate a language that is out of control and self-subverting. The change of mood is pointed up as the duck passage moves to a memory of having used chicken droppings for garden plants. These constituted "a powerful ingredient that / through the delicacies of floral / transfiguration / makes tasty gravy" (p. 254). Ammons, earlier repelled by biological facts, is now himself able to transfigure them into the palatable. Notice how "floral" operates here, as opposed to the effect of the "microfloral" used in the "bloomers" passage.

Wayward as the matter it now takes up, the poem goes on to speak of an instance of sexual perversion. We are warned to avoid devices and practices "that lead gradually away / from picnic tables, / the trivial fluvial fumes of sunday braziers" (p. 255). The upholding of Sunday cookouts as the norm, the alternative to sexual perversions, seems to be done tongue in cheek, but perhaps not completely so. Ammons showed a streak of social conservatism in

Tape, and his endorsement of family life, which is what the picnic tables and braziers suggest, should not be dismissed as simply ironic. Moreover, what the stanza may really amount to is an admonition to *himself* to move in "approved channels"—his treatment of sex earlier in the poem, in its preoccupation with women as bearers of bacilli, had a perversity of its own; he had considered things too curiously.

There may also be a self-rebuke in the poem when, changing focus once again, it becomes concerned with Ammons' position as a poet. Specifying his age as forty-two, he finds that others have advanced beyond him; now he is going to make *his* move. He may be confronting and rejecting his Doppelgänger, in the anecdote he tells about a man under a soaking elm tree (he himself was getting pleasure soaking under that tree). He shows disgust with the man, who is "so needy something's rotten" (p. 256). Like the humor of Ammons' sequence of poems beginning "I can tell you what I need is," the disgust may be part of an attempted purging of self-pity he has discovered within himself. But if this is the case, his feelings are not confined to disgust; he shows that here too he can be humorous, as he declares his emergence as a poet.

Summer Session, finally meeting the expectation set up by the title, comes to focus, if only briefly, on Ammons' activities as a teacher of writing (it gave indication of doing so earlier, but instantly dropped the subject). At this point (p. 257), *Summer Session* seems to be in good spirits. But it takes a sudden plunge; having finally arrived at the teaching of verse writing, it appears to belittle poetry. The phrase "down the drains," used earlier in the dark consideration of vaginal bacteria, is now echoed in the words "down this drain," which initiates a confused imaging of glut and destruction. Poems, the poem seems to be implying, are part of a motley stream of things set down on paper, and are without redeeming power: "imagination's / winding no scraps up into / windy transfigurations" (p. 258). Joining the stream of paper is a dreadful sundry, including engorged ticks, dirty rats, rust, pus, snot, "wound weepage," and "wart-juice" (p. 258). This listing, infused with disgust, and reminiscent of Pound's "Hell Cantos," is ironically set off by the lines that follow, made up of the cheerful choices in advertising copy directed at "families with a lot of living to do" (p. 258). Then we and / or Ammons' students are told to discover for ourselves "where / the problems are" and to "amass / alternative strategies" (p. 259). This cool advice seems to come out of nowhere, after the horrific vision of ticks, pus, and snot.

Still, Ammons will not be fixed in that vision. Though the imagination may produce no windy transfigurations, it is capable of some achievements, and Ammons intends to try for them, to be at least a small wind: "I scribble, baby, I mean / I breeze on" (p. 259). Also, the scientific apprehension of the world still has the power to attract him: "to a cartographer / part of Pennsylvania's a broken record: / curving grooves & ridges in / visual music" (p. 259). In addition, there is his capacity for tender concern with the small. He notes a baby robin that has been wet all day, and thinks that if the weather were dry, the bird might acquire some ability to fly.

In the poem's final stanza, Ammons defines his functions as a teacher:

> here are the 18-year-old
> seedbeds & the
> 19-year-old fertilizers:
> they have come for a summer session:
> knowledge is to be my insemination:
> I grant it them as one grants flesh
> the large white needle:
> what shall I tell those who are
> nervous,
> too tender for needles, the
> splitting of irridescent tendons:
> oh I tell them nothing can realize
> them, nothing ruin them
> like the poundage of pure self:
> with my trivia
> I'll dispense dignity, a sense of office,
> formality they can define themselves against:
> the head is my sphere:
> I'll look significant as I deal with
> mere wires of light, ghosts of
> cells, working there. (p. 260)

A kind of poise is achieved here, the conflicting elements of the stanza, and of the poem, working into a synthesis, though one not without self-irony. The biological-agricultural metaphors designating the students seem, on first reading, reductive, but perhaps are meant to recall the honored ability of a species to maintain shape and flow, to "hold / figuration in the cast seed." The needle simile for the conveying of knowledge joins up with the earlier characterization of knowledge as painful, that which "shivers / into the blood stream." But the administering of the needle is qualified by the poet-teacher's worrying about some students' ability to withstand the pain; they become, in effect, joined with the baby robin as beings who elicit his sympathy and concern. The "poundage" of the self functions as two metaphors reinforcing each other, one referring to weight, the other to hammering or striking. They tell us that the self is burdensome or hurtful to itself, perhaps (among other reasons) because of such dark visions as the self of the poem calls up. But the weight-hammer is seen as creative as well as destructive. Although Ammons feels that as a teacher he can convey nothing of importance to his students, only "trivia," he believes he can represent the poet as a dignified man with a high vocation. While, in reality, he considers the workings of his mind as insubstantial, he can convey the impression of significance.

The picture of the poet-teacher that we get here is ironic, not only in itself, but in relation to the poem as a whole. For there is certainly irony in the notion of this poet conveying formality and dignity, when his poem has been so loose in structure and so uninhibited in expression, and when he has been so undignified at one point as to promise that he will "strip and shit" (p. 257). That is to say, there is a sharp discrepancy not only between the elevated persona Ammons presents to his students and the actual self-image of the concluding stanza, but between that persona and the I of the entire poem (more about this in a moment).

On the other hand, the "mere wires of light, ghosts of / cells" by which Ammons apparently dismisses the workings of his head, calls up an earlier passage which resists such self-diminution, a passage which links the "ghosts" of memories to "essences" finer than light ([p. 249]—admittedly, there is something ambiguous about this passage). Also, while the poet may have pounded himself, there is a sense of genuine self-acceptance, of coming to rest, in the last lines of the poem, generated by the *sphere-there* rhyme (which echoes and qualifies the self-denigration of *mere*). Terminal rhyme is so rare in Ammons as to take on particular force when it appears, even in slant form.

At one point in *Summer Session*, Ammons states that "those in the height . . . / . . . hate / wide . . . disparities" (p. 257). It is not clear who "those" are. It *is* clear that this poem has no such hatred, compounding itself of wide disparities, both of subject matter and tone. *Summer Session* (like "Spiel") has a predilection for "widest play," play made possible by the nothingness posited by the poem (pp. 249 - 50). Life, it tells us, "adds up / to exactly nothing" (p. 256), and perhaps the poem is implicitly adopting an aesthetic based on this, namely, that it can play as it wants, and that this play need not add up to anything. The poem is a vehicle for the variety of its maker's concerns and moods. It enters, with its shifting, uninhibited diction, into the spirit of the moment. Continuously arresting in its individual stanzas, with their use of language and detail, it resists being gathered into a structure, and so is troubling, at least for this reader.

But perhaps *Summer Session* does possess a particular impulse, one that can be seen as linking many, if not all, of its stanzas. That impulse can be defined as one of unmasking. Possessing initially a double authority, as poet and as teacher, Ammons has his poem reveal the self behind the official facade, a being who is not invariably controlled, reasonable, adult, but one who can be furious, perverse, morbid, silly, abusive, gross, disgusted. In this sense *Summer Session* can be taken as a piece of confessional poetry. Also, remembering that it was originally entitled *Summer Session 1968*, we can see it as coming out of a period in which many academics were questioning their own authority, and attempting to diminish the traditional distance between teacher and student. While Ammons assumes a traditional stance at the end of the poem vis-à-vis his students, it comes down to the putting on of a mask by a man who has already revealed himself, and at length, as a creature other than the formal and dignified presence of the classroom.

IV   Pray Without Ceasing

Pray Without Ceasing ranges in reference from outer space to microflora, from ancient Egypt to the Vietnamese War. Its modes include an anguished quotation from Trismegistus, instructions for operating machines in a laundromat, lists of words and phrases having a particular word or syllable in common, and jingles about a little phony named Dapple Gray. We might almost regard it as parodying the pastiche technique of the modernist long poem (*The Waste Land, The Cantos, The Bridge, Paterson*). But it has little of the lightheartedness or detachment of parody. Its discontinuities are its own, not playful takeoffs on other poems. One hopes that one's discoveries of relationships among its parts are not merely factitious, the results of a kind of critical gerrymandering. But the work does seem to go one step beyond Stevens' prescription that a poem should resist the intelligence almost successfully.

Ammons' Muse, his Pegasus, is conceived of in the poem as a minor one perhaps, but unruly, not open to control. This is what I take to be the significance of the two separate quatrains about Dapple Gray. In the first of these, Ammons tells us that "every time I had him, / he tried to get away" (*D*, 84). Parallel to this are the lines of the second, "when I tried to trim him, / he had a lot to bray" (*D*, 88). Moreover, the poem appears to defend its disorder against those who would build a false "unity of walls"; it favors instead letting "weeds and grasses move in among a / scattering" (*D*, 96; the "weeds" here and the "rubble" that comes a few lines before should be compared with those same terms as they appear in "High and Low").

According to the poem, imposing, ordered structures can only dissolve in the face of complexity. So, espousing what others might call the imitative fallacy, Ammons, with a mixture of insouciance, defiance, and humility, appears to justify the disjointedness of his verse by seeing it as reflecting the unmanageable variety and complexity of reality. Not wishing to build sleek, rational structures, Ammons portrays himself as a scrounger at the edges of junkyards (reminding us of Stevens' "The Man on the Dump"), wondering if he can make his song out of "boggy garbage, / fly swarms, lamb bones, and rust-floral / cans" (*D*, 97).

Advocating swirl and a sense of how complex things are, Ammons *wants* the world to be impenetrable, to defy ordering and knowledge. The poem associates "a mastery of oceans" with death (*D*, 88), and Ammons desires mystery, not mastery. On the other hand, he wishes to believe in some ordering principle, some coherence behind the motion, if only the motion of his poem. If he does not understand in confronting mystery, he hopes he may be understood. Moreover, it does not matter what he says because the motions by which he moves "manifest / merely a deeper congruence / where the structures are" (*D*, 96). It is not clear, to this reader at least, whether the structures in question are those of his sensibility or those of reality, or both.

Pray Without Ceasing is not confined to issues of form or structure (though we are not yet done with those issues). The poem is largely fueled by powerful feelings coming mainly out of its awareness of suffering and death, locating these in, among other places, ancient Egypt and, by implication, modern Vietnam. Ammons seems uncomfortable with the use of the latter, an untypical allusion to current events, and he suggests, if I read him correctly, that there is something spurious about his attempt to make a connection with such material (D, 95 - 96). Elsewhere, more characteristically, he gazes at the cosmos, and experiences terror (D, 94). But the sources of pain can be found closer to home than ancient Egypt or modern Vietnam or outer space; as he says, his "acquaintance / with grief is / intimate" (D, 83). It is a grief springing from past losses and from anticipation. He fears his *own* death, thinking about the possibility of a heart attack (D, 91).

There is no denying or obliterating the painful; it is a fundamental given, an "absolute" (D, 95). While nature may afford a refuge from pain, its place in the poem is small, and it is somewhat disappointing. During an excursion into the woods at the beginning of spring, hundreds of plants are seen, "but few bloomers" (D, 86).

In places, sex appears more promising than nature as a refuge: "don't snatch & grab: grab snatch: / . . . / when a system of two bodies / charges and discharges itself / it's peaceful as tulips" (D, 97). But sex figures as more than sex here; it is related to the poem's aesthetic stance (in analyzing *Pray Without Ceasing* it is necessary to keep returning to this). For sex, presumably an instance of the irrational, is implicitly associated with a "directed unity" (D, 81) which is opposed to the mistaken direction of rationality, the building of massive, ordered structures, such as those created by Hegel or Milton. (The former is named directly; the latter enters the poem via a pun, "milt on / the levees of rationality" (D, 81), which I take as pointing to the triumph of sex—"milt" denotes the male fish's generative organs or their secretion—over structures ["levees"] designed to hold back the turbulent complexity of existence.)[8]

But *Pray Without Ceasing* is not entirely comfortable in its affirmation of sex. A passage that begins with a pleasurable sexual entry proceeds to give us this: "O rose / the microflora along your hinder walls / are fast bloomers" (D, 83 - 84). We have here, in what might be considered a variation on Blake's sick rose, a clinical view of the female genitalia as a repository of bacteria (see *Summer Session*). The lines acquire additional force when we come upon the "few bloomers," noted earlier, which refer to spring flowers. We have fast bloomers where there should be none, few bloomers where there should be many. The stanza of the fast bloomers appears determined to conclude insouciantly, using lighthearted alliteration and wordplay (D, 84), but something goes awry. Sex apparently fails here as a relief from intimate acquaintance with grief.

Another qualification of the power of sex to comfort the troubled mind of the poem may be found, operating somewhat indirectly, in a section that begins with instructions for using the washer in a laundromat (*D*, 89). These instructions, suggestive of sex, are followed by a word list in which "cock" is the featured term. This in turn is followed by instructions for dry cleaning. Both sets of instructions are precise and sure (the last term in the word list is "cocksure"). But as the poem proceeds, notice is taken of objects which can be spoiled by the cleaning process or which are impervious to it. Immediately after this comes a passage on heart attack, which speaks of how the cardiac artery "pops" ("pop" figured as the central term in an earlier word list). Putting these materials together, we can say that the poem moves from a playful suggestion of sex, implied in a form that indicates sureness and control, to an area where objects begin to elude our control, and finally to where the body itself, through a minimal action ("pops"), goes its own, disastrous way. The sequence that started with the suggestion of sex ends with death.

Not only does the poem diminish the power of sex that it originally affirmed, it also questions that which it associates with sex and espouses, namely, antirationality. In the middle of a passage denigrating "buildings of rationality," it notes that "anti-rationality only makes another / kind of thrust" (*D*, 89).[9] In what could be taken as a complementary passage, theorizing seems to be treated honorifically (*D*, 97). In short, the affirmations of sex and antirationality are not permitted to go unchallenged.

That one source of the poem's troubled sensibility is middle age is indicated by a series of lines which employ a wave as a metaphor. As the wave moves in and builds in height it reaches a condition of "maximum / organization," this representing life at its peak. Then "one is / forty & hollow." Optimum shape is lost to this hollow. That there is a seemingly compensatory gain, or that there will be another wave, is of little consolation. What has been achieved appears to be regarded lightly ("dip it and ship it" [*D*, 93]).

Ammons is also oppressed by less personal considerations, by what his scientific knowledge has brought him, namely, a sense of the obliteration of distinctions toward which the physics of the universe is moving, "the spurt for / equilibrium" (*D*, 93). The poem first responds to its vision of homogenization by turning to the identity, the individuation ("root, / bark, leaf must make a walnut") embraced in poems like "Risks and Possibilities" and "Identity." But then, through the figure of a saint, there is a swerve toward the kind of renunciation of earthly life that was so prominent in *Ommateum* (but not in later volumes). Here there seems to be an ambivalence toward such renunciation, but that it is entertained at all is a symptom of the poem's consciousness of temporal woes. The image of the ascending, "skinny" saint may be an embodiment of the "something / thin & high," mentioned earlier in the poem, that cuts through "terror, pity, grief, death" (*D*, 82). This something "makes no difference of difference" (*D*, 83), hence is similar to the forces that obliterate distinctions. To do away with pain one must achieve on an individual, voluntary basis, what ultimately will be done universally, namely, the wiping out of life's multiplicity and individuation.

A recourse available to Ammons, other than a complete turning away from this world, is the conversion of his supposedly wasted life to usefulness through language (*D*, 85). Words may be said to constitute his "stock in trade" (*D*, 80), the first phrase in the first of the poem's word lists, lists that testify to a fascination with language per se. While Ammons' delight in the patterns or echoes arising from words is not commensurate with the sources of oppression in *Pray Without Ceasing*, language for him can bulk large enough to count. He speaks at one point of a "redeeming / light, / the light in the head / of language in motion" (*D*, 92). Language can engage the oppressive, and can render pain endurable. The poem ends with an image that can be regarded as a joining of language and pain—"aching out tongues" (*D*, 98). In context this is especially striking, because of the way it concludes an important strain of the poem, one related to a larger pattern in Ammons' works.

I noted in Chapter 4 that there is in the poems a pattern of simultaneous "highs" and "lows" (or ascents and descents) signaling moments of particular felicity. *Pray Without Ceasing* begins with precisely such a moment:

> I hear the low falling from the
> highlands of hog-pasture, a music
> of spheres, a couple. . . . (*D*, 80)

The joining of "low" and "high," the "couple," is heightened by the juxtaposition of the homely "hog-pasture" with the grand, traditional image of the music of the spheres. But where in other instances the euphoric high-low conjunction goes unchallenged, the linkage in these lines is immediately subjected to dissolution, Ammons saying that "whatever is / done is to be / undone," and asking to be called "down from the / high places" (*D*, 80). The privileged condition that has been named in the poem's opening lines may well be considered a "high place." If so, the poet wishes to be removed therefrom; as a matter of fact, in the very act of calling for that removal he effects it, by separating low ("down") from high. The original couple has been undone.[10] Moreover, when "couple" next appears in the poem, it does so in a very different way, in this tiny, punning stanza: "a pararox [*sic*], couple achers: the / real estate of the imagination . . ." (*D*, 82). The domain of the imagination, its (rocky?) *acre*age, is a restricted realm of aches. So that where "couple" previously figured in the poem's euphoric opening, its happy joining of opposites, it is now associated with oppressive paradox and pain.

On the last page of the poem we get other instances of highs and lows, but these do not constitute a return to what we had at the beginning. (If anything, they sustain in one way or another the undoing of the original synthesis.) In the first example, apart from the fact that the high, in the form of mental "skyscrapers," has been tainted by the poem's earlier treatment of buildings of rationality, the syntax and phrasing are such that the relationship between high and low is muddy, as opposed to the clear, simultaneous presence of opposites in other high-low examples. In the second instance of high and low, the two are clearly separated:

>   . . . damp
> heat built
> and rose through the golden towered afternoon,
>
> broke finally into motion, as of
> descent, rain beating
> straight down
> between racks of thunder. . . . (*D*, 98)

The downward movement, following what seems to be both an attractive and oppressive buildup, brings to mind the self-injunction of the poem's second stanza: "call me down from the high places" (*D*, 80).

Pray Without Ceasing concludes:

> we found hailstones in the grass
> and ate them to cool:

        spurred stones
        with interior milkwhite halos,
        an arrested sprangling:
        the high hard water
        melted
        aching out tongues.

What we have here are objects from on high, from the pure and
heavenly ("milkwhite halos"). They are frozen, fixed, until, having
come down from the high places, they are joined to the human, and
thereby associated with process, language, and pain.

As I read *Pray Without Ceasing*, then, it displays a self-
chastening on Ammons' part, a renunciation of resting in the kind
of experience designated by the poem's opening. Such euphoric,
static moments, dramatized by high and low coexisting, are too
removed, too special. The commitment here is to downward motion, which, elsewhere in Ammons usually a matter of accepting
multiplicity, is here a matter of acknowledging the sources of grief.
To pray without ceasing may be to speak language that recognizes
the painfulness and mutability of things, confronting head-on the
kinds of experience *Tape for the Turn of the Year* was reluctant to
acknowledge.

V   Extremes and Moderations

Calling itself a "poem or prose-poem" (p. 339), *Extremes and
Moderations* falls somewhere between the expository mode of *Essay
on Poetics* and the emotional expressiveness of *Summer Session*.
Like the former work, *Extremes* is composed mostly of long-line
stanzas of equal length, with some departures from the basic form,
including, as in *Essay*, a poem-within-a-poem about an elm tree. It
is more coherent than *Essay*, and certainly more so than *Pray
Without Ceasing* and *Summer Session*. It focuses steadily on two
related subjects: first, extreme and moderate forces or conditions,
principally in nature, and, second, man's upsetting the balance of
nature.

But before *Extremes* settles down to dealing with these, it seems
to indicate that it will be about everything, in an opening stanza
whose omnivorous, rapid lines jump from sailing to the theater to
electronics to the circus. The poem even speaks of a "world-
replacing world / . . . lesser than but more outspoken" (pp. 328 -
29), which I take to be the world of words the work intends to
create.

Then *Extremes* suddenly seems to shrink to an essay about its own poetics, its own stanzaic unfolding. Ammons speaks of his stanza form as a "lattice" permitting flow, and thinks of the poem moving down the page as well as across it (although the long lines of the work highlight the latter movement). He continues:

> . . . my ideal's a cold
> clod clam calm, clam contained, nevertheless active in the
> digestion, capable of dietary mirth, the sudden whisk, nearly
> rollably spherical. . . . (p. 329)

One ventures to guess that the "ideal" here, formulated as a joking tongue-twister, is a tightly structured but lively lyric. The joking "cold / clod clam calm" is characterized by its blatant cohesiveness of sound, if not of sense, with the second and fourth words generated by spelling inversions of the first and third terms, respectively. The phrase itself is highly "contained," and in a sense nearly "spherical," curving back on itself. But the formulation of Ammons' "ideal" in such a phrase is self-undermining, mocking the cold, contained quality supposedly being affirmed. What really draws him is indicated by the lines following immediately on those given above:

> . . . ah, but friends, to be turned
>
> loose on an accurate impulse! how handsome the stanzas are
> beginning to look, open to the total acceptance, fracturing into
> delight, tugging down the broad sweep, thrashing it into
> particulars (within boundaries). . . . (p. 329)

Like the poem's opening stanza, this indicates an attraction to a broad inclusiveness, a largeness of form. But while there is pleasure in turning loose, there is also a curbing consideration: "diversity . . . / . . . is not ever pleasing." Also, the poem does claim for itself a "central impulse" (p. 329). In fact, as already noted, *Extremes and Moderations* will flow its length through relatively narrow channels, though hardly denying itself a diversity of illustrative materials, ranging from a marble bench in the poet's backyard to lightning and icebergs, thereby demonstrating its contention that "there's / plenty around for the mind to dwell on" (p. 330).

The marble bench serves to announce Ammons' first major theme. Never as warm or as cold as the surrounding air, it serves as a moderating influence. Ostensibly fixed, it is actually made up,

Ammons points out, mindful of its atomic structure, of "all moving parts" (p. 330). Virtually all the moderating forces he deals with in the poem involve motion or, in the terminology of the work, "circulations." (Extremes are seen as triggering motions, sometimes taking the form of circulations themselves.) Mechanisms evolved over millions of years, these circulations have made for us an earth "deliciously / habitable" (p. 334). The interplay of extreme and moderation in nature, the one sometimes becoming or producing the other, also elicits gratitude and marveling from Ammons (as well as the playful announcement at one point that he is going to introduce a moderate extreme [p. 331]). In this poem, as in other of his works, the functionings of the world are regarded as wonderful. He does have some troubling thoughts about the operations of nature causing harm to itself or human beings, but, in his poem-within-a-poem about the elm, he arrives at an acceptance of this.

Cutting across the miraculous and generally beneficent complex of extremes and moderations in nature are the activities of man. He has caused nature to circulate his industrial refuse. The pollutants he has produced through his own extreme, his attempt to exploit and control the earth, may prove too much for the diffusive powers of nature's moderating forces. These observations are by now commonplace, but Ammons gives them striking formulation:

> . . . an oil slick covers every inch
>
> of ocean surface: at the poles pilots see in the contrast the
> sullied air's worldwide: because of the circulations, water can
> never be picked up for use except from its usages, where what
> has gone in is not measured or determined: extreme calls to
>
> extreme and moderation is losing its quality, its effect: the
> artificial has taken on the complication of the natural. . . . (p. 340)

If man has overburdened earth's moderating circulations, he has also attempted to deny or freeze them. Ammons, taking off from his modern, scientific knowledge of circulations, but adopting an age-old mode, the voice of the prophet, condemns the city as an artifact that shuts out circulations. He recalls its true parentage, the glacier its mother, "the currents of the deep" its father. (This treatment of the city might be compared to Charles Olson's treatment of Gloucester in *Maximus Poems IV, V, VI*). He urges women to enter the currents, men to plunge "into the ecstasy of rapids." The prophetic voice breaks down temporarily into self-consciousness and sophistication, but is able to resume, Ammons addressing us as "children of the light: of seasons, moons, apples, berries, / grain," saying "come out, I cry, into / your parentage, your established natures" (p. 335).

Still, Ammons does not seem comfortable using this voice, and without even waiting for a new stanza, he says, immediately after the words just quoted:

> I went out and pulled a

> few weeds in the lawn: you probably think I was getting goofy
> or scared: it was just another show: as the mystic said, it's
> all one to me. . . . (p. 336)

Though the injunction to immerse in currents does seem a bit forced, Ammons imitating somebody else (Lawrence?), the prophetic passage does have power, and it is disturbing that Ammons is willing to disavow it so totally and with a gag (which also seem to mock his concern with the One and the Many). Why write the passage in the first place if it is to be thus dismissed?[11]

But the ecological concern of the poem seems genuine, deeply felt, though Ammons does not fall into unrelieved pessimism or condemnation. There is a note of cheer in these wonderful lines:

> . . . the little patch
> of wildwoods out behind my backhedge is even now squeaky and

> chirpy with birds and the day is as clear as a missing windowpane:
> the clouds are few, large, and vastly white: the air has no
> smell and the shade of trees is sharp. . . . (p. 337)

Later in the poem, taking the large view, Ammons wryly acknowledges that ruin and destruction are the fate of the planet whatever we do, through forces beyond those of man or earth.

Still, man has left his terrible mark, and Ammons tells us that this poem seems to him the last one "written to the world / before its freshness capsizes and sinks into the slush" (p. 340). The final passage of the work focuses on what we are perpetrating against our home, and the mood is grim, not really relieved by the playful use of one of the title words: "if contaminated / water forces me to the extreme purification of bottled or distilled / water, the extreme will be costly . . ." (p. 341).

Near the end of *Extremes and Moderations,* Ammons
characterizes the poem as a harmless device, and associates it with
sex, which he sees as "innocent, non-destructive" (p. 341), in contrast, presumably, to the devices or practices of the world destructive of its ecology. But earlier, the poem, even while sounding
modest, seemed to be making more of a case for itself. Speaking of
requesting rain during a time of drought, Ammons had stated that
"saying doesn't do any good but it doesn't / hurt: aligns the psychic
forces with the natural" (p. 339). If we interpret "saying" as not
simply the request for rain, but as the poem itself, then the intended function of *Extremes and Moderations* can be taken as giving or restoring to us a sense of how the world works, and making us
share Ammons' wonder and reverence as he contemplates that
working. When he calls *Extremes and Moderations* harmless, he
says he is letting "the world / breeze unobstructed through" it (p.
341). The metaphor is questionable. Language inevitably refracts,
but it does so here to exhibit appreciatively our earth's sustaining
circulations.

VI Hibernaculum

Hibernaculum's title word signifies a protective case or covering
for winter, housing either plant or animal life; it can also mean the
winter quarters of a hibernating animal. In either case it suggests a
cozy enclosure of some kind. But there is little sense of enclosure
offered by the construction of the poem itself. While each of its one
hundred and twelve sections (every one of which consists of three
nonrhyming tercets) is formally marked off by Arabic numbering,
most of these divisions are made to spill over their boundaries, joining up with the succeeding sections. There is no full stop in the
poem before its final word. Moreover, within a given stanza of a
section, Ammons is likely to effect a startling change in subject
matter. Thus, the sections function only as pseudoenclosures, with
the stanzas themselves frequently failing to encapsulate a
homogeneous substance. (The discontinuity *within* stanzas combined with the continuity *between* stanzas can also be found in
Essay on Poetics and *Extremes and Moderations.*)

Still, the poem as a whole may have been conceived by Ammons
as a winter self-covering, though not for the purpose of hibernation.
Internal evidence suggests that much of it was written during a
December-January stretch, and it can be seen as a project by which

Ammons kept himself mentally warm and poetically active. There are some indications that the poem was willed, if not into being, then into continuation. But it is a remarkable work, much finer than that other winter work of the will, *Tape for the Turn of the Year*. It does not, as *Tape* does, take "long / uninteresting walks" so that we can "experience / vacancy" (*T*, 205). Keeping its flow going "in order to hope he will / say something he means" (p. 368), Ammons acknowledges that though the poem may not necessarily be able to make sense of the world, it is obliged, as it moves along, to be interesting: "procedure's the only procedure: if things don't add / up, they must interest at every moment" (p. 387).

What is the poem about? A better question might be: what isn't it about? Ammons himself seems to recognize this. He says:

> . . . if there is to be
> no principle of inclusion, then, at least, there ought
>
> to be a principle of exclusion, for to go with a maw at
> the world as if to chew it up and spit
> it out again as one's own is to trifle with terrible
>
> affairs. . . . (pp. 386 - 87)

Ammons comically agrees to omit, among other things, the "transmutations and permutations of / Chinese civilization" (a mischievous allusion, perhaps, to Pound's omnivorous *Cantos*, with their sections of Chinese history), "most, / if not all, of the Amazon basin," and nearly all of the earth's population (p. 387).

These hardly restrictive exclusions are stated very late in the poem, which has ranged uninhibitedly, meriting the adjective it coins, "scopy" (p. 366). As we read it, the poem seems open to anything Ammons can think of, which is a great deal. *Hibernaculum* speaks of "a poem variable as a dying man, willing to try anything" (p. 364), and this amounts to a self-description. But much of it is drawn to certain familiar themes: the One and the Many (or unity and multiplicity, center and periphery), the wondrous mechanisms of the physical and biological worlds, poetry, form and motion, the great in the small.

Besides these, there are two principal themes, intersecting at a number of points: giving and nothingness. One way in which giving operates in the poem is in the sense of a forced yielding up. We are, through death, made to surrender the precious things of this world.

But the poem wishes to rescue giving from the realm of the compulsory, to make it voluntary. This giving can take the form of love, and of surrender to the moment that must pass. Such giving is linked both to total satisfaction and to nothingness ("zero" [p. 354]).

Another form of giving, also fated to disappear into nothingness (the latter will presently be treated in itself), is Ammons' presenting his art to us. Out of his background and experiences, "New Hope Elementary School, assorted / mothers and fathers," etc., he wishes "to furnish forth energy," though he knows he "can't give all that back . . . / . . . anyway it's just giving / nothing to nothing" (p. 360).

While *Hibernaculum* is hardly Christian in its assumptions, it considers St. Francis as a possible, if formidable, model of giving (p. 363). This occurs immediately after lines in which Ammons speaks of making himself the center of his world. The example of St. Francis works against such an act, and it is a Franciscan strain that is affirmed later in the poem, when the poet finds satisfaction in the relinquishment of will, the surrender of self to the flow of things: "I exist by just so much as I am will-lessly borne / along"; "by just / so much as I have given up, I am sustained" (pp. 370 - 371). But this quiescence is not allowed to go unqualified, for immediately after making this last statement Ammons gives us a repulsive image: "finally / the boat bumps solid, sucks the surface tit, and, bloated, drowns" (p. 371).

This is death, one form of nothingness in the poem. What we come from is also nothingness; our passage is "from zero to zero" (p. 353). Nothingness is also what the poet's quest comes down to (pp. 372, 373). But this pervasive sense of nothingness, the conclusion that "it all adds up to zero" (p. 356) or that "the sum of everything's nothing" (p. 379), does not necessarily produce gloom and despair throughout the poem. The nothingness of *Hibernaculum*, akin to that of existentialism (and adumbrated in *Summer Session*), is the single "absolute," one that guarantees freedom, the freedom of each thing to be, and to find its significance simply in its being. Nothingness "is really the point of lovely liberation, when / gloriously every object in and on earth becomes just / itself" (pp. 379 - 80). The sensibility here is like that of Stevens in "Sunday Morning" and other poems. Nothingness gives us the world in its wonderful multiplicity, "manifold with things and beings" (p. 380). This is the antithesis of the nothingness Ammons sometimes associates with the One.

But while nothingness may, paradoxically, be the source of a wonderful plenitude, that plenitude is all too mortal. As we go "from zero to zero we / pass through magnificence too shatterable" (p. 353). In another formulation of this, Ammons moves with shocking swiftness from the abundance generated by the void to the total disappearance of that abundance:

> . . .the void is the
>
> birthplace of finches, gyrfalcons, juncos (a specialty),
> snowy egrets, woodcocks, hummingbirds, crows, jays,
> wood ducks, warblers, titmice, and the end of everything. . . . (p. 373)

In a yet darker passage there is a vision of bleakness and *dreck:* " I see a world made, unmade, and made again / and I hear crying either way . . . / . . . I see grime, just grime, grain, / grit, grist" (p. 353).

Such gloomy moments are in tension with those where Ammons is able to derive satisfaction from the world. The resulting ambivalence of the poem has been anticipated by a statement, early in the work, of a double vision of things, introduced by a peculiar, unstable compound of fear and acquiescence:

> . . . I am alarmed with acceptance:nothing
>
> made right could have been made this way, and nothing
> made otherwise could have been made right: nothing can
> be made to make it right. . . . (p. 353)

The last assertion here tips toward the pessimistic, but the poem does not adopt that as its dominant tone. For example, we can set against the observation that "nothing can be made to make it right" the following: "I can't / help thinking that what we have is right enough, the / core of the galaxy . . . / . . . toads, picnic tables, morning glories, firs afire" (p. 377). The interwoven sounds of "firs afire" come as the climax to a passage which is a wonderful variation on the Heraclitean vision of all things being on fire, a vision that Ammons seems to find entrancing. To be sure, we move immediately from the fiery trees to a section which gloomily pictures the world as a circus shut down. But this only illustrates the poem's refusal to rest in a particular attitude. It continually changes its tone as well as its subject matter.

It can change sharply its scope or its level as well. Thus, *Hibernaculum* jumps from speaking of the assumptions that govern the contemporary young to describing a trip taken to purchase a Christmas tree, from consideration of the void to a dream about Edna St. Vincent Millay, from thoughts about nothingness and freedom to the breakdown of a car part. But despite the variety of subject matter, tone, and scope, we do not find, by and large, the unfortunate disjunctions of language I have pointed to in *Tape for the Turn of the Year*. (Perhaps *Tape* should be seen, at this point in Ammons' career, not as the prelude to the short, hard, rich lyrics it spoke of, but as a necessary warm-up for the more accomplished long poems that came later.) Ammons' diction in *Hibernaculum* ranges widely, but functions in a supple way, as in the following:

> work's never done: the difficult work of dying
> remains, remains, and remains: a brain lobe squdging
> against the skull, a soggy kidney, a little vessel
>
> smartly plugged: wrestling with one—or those—until
> the far-feared quietus comes bulby, floating glimmer-wobbling
> to pop. . . . (pp. 369 - 70)

The poem's language fulfills the ideal, proposed in *Tape*, of an idiom that could take in all sorts of material without fracturing, that would "not be completely / outfaced / by the prosaic / & not be inadequate / to the surges" (*T*, 144). We find both the prosaic and the surges in *Hibernaculum*. The poem is capable of moving from one to the other, and of shifting its diction without jarring us, as in the following:

>   . . . let's join to the deepest slowing,
> turn the deepest dark into touch, gape, pumping, at the
>
> dark beyond reach: afterwards, shoveling the driveway,
> warming up the coffee, going to the grocery store, opening
> the cookie jar, washing, shaving, vacuuming, looking out
>
> the window at the perilously afflicted, that is, snow-loaded
> bent evergreens, watching the pheasants walking across
> the yard, plopping up belly-deep in snow. . . . (p. 355)

We go from the intensity of sex, an outer boundary of experience, to the mundane acts that fill our days, to the view through the window of both pathetic trees and humorous birds, in language that is never forced or fractured.

Whatever surges there are in *Hibernaculum,* whatever affirmations or syntheses, the poem does not come to rest in any of them. It is committed to its process of unfolding more than to some final resolution or illumination. Its outrageous opening lines about the chewing of a cud (quoted in Chapter 4, p. 72) may be intended as a comment on its own nature. That is, the poem may be regarded as an extended act of *rumination,* "a repeating of / gently repeating motions, blissful slobber-spun webs" (p. 351). This is a comic conception of the poem's enterprise, but we need not assume that that enterprise is simply being mocked. In a later section, Ammons voices his belief that when the mind becomes "fully born, / it will be another earth, just like / the earth, but visionary, earth luminous with sight" (p. 367). It will have all the earth's typographical features and processes. After predicting this, *Hibernaculum* goes on to ask why a certain "he" writes poems. This "he," I believe, can be taken as "I," that is Ammons himself.[12] The juxtaposition of the statement about the mind and the question of the motive for writing poems is suggestive. It encourages us to say that *Hibernaculum* is intended as a work that moves toward the full birth of the mind, toward the assimilation, by the contemplative consciousness, of the richness of the world.

VII   Sphere: The Form of a Motion

Sphere: The Form of a Motion, Ammons' latest long work, is second only to *Tape for the Turn of the Year* in length. In form it is most like *Hibernaculum,* consisting of one hundred and fifty-five numbered sections, each section comprised of a fixed quantity of long-line tercets (four to *Hibernaculum's* three), with no full stop, that is, no period, provided before the very end; here, too, there is a heavy reliance on colons to mark off units of thought. Again as with *Hibernaculum,* the rigidity of external form is strongly counterpointed by the tendency of the sections, once we get past the first half-dozen pages, to spill over their ostensible boundaries, and by Ammons' feeling free to shift subject matter abruptly within a given stanza. As he himself says in the poem, "I do not smooth into groups" (*S,* 16).

This statement is part of the explicit resistance or hostility to structure which functions as a major motif of the poem (as is the case in *Pray Without Ceasing*). That is, *Sphere* is often, in a self-justifying way, about its own poetics, its unfolding as a linear mode. Late in the work, Ammons declares himself "sick of good poems, all those little rondures / splendidly brought off, painted gourds on a shelf" (*S*, 72). The shapeliness or structure suggested by "rondures" is thus associated with minor accomplishment. These lines amount to a stronger version of what Ammons says in an early section of *Sphere*, "I / never did like anything too well done" (*S*, 4).[13] His is one of those minds he cites that are "nervous of structures" (*S*, 72). He lets us know this both with brisk concision—"I don't want shape" (*S*, 45)—and with humorous elaboration, in a passage that may owe a little to Stevens' "The Man on the Dump" as well as Wilbur's "Junk." Here he tells us he wants "to be declared a natural disaster area," to be a "junkyard where my awkwardnesses may show," and "where charlatan rationality comes / to warp, where the smooth finishes bubble and perk . . ." (*S*, 68).

The prejudice against neat shape or form in poetry is undoubtedly related to Ammons' sense that in natural phenomena "the shapes nearest shapelessness awe us most, suggest / the god" (*S*, 16). A log, "rigid with shape," is regarded by him as "trivial" (*S*, 16). The one concession that he makes to shape in the poem, his long-line stanza form (what I take him to mean when he refers to "this measure"), is "the log the stream flows against / for a whole year" (*S*, 28). The passive position to which this assigns the log or stanza is instructive. That stanza allows the poem's matter to flow against it, or better, though it, functioning like the self-designated "lattice work" of *Extremes and Moderations* (just after the reference to the log and the stream, Ammons refers to the "mesh" of his measure [*S*, 28]). The materials of "this open form" are entrusted with finding their own "running self-concisions and expansions" (*S*, 39), in a passage where "open form" may also refer to the world itself. Ammons envisions a form in which "many structures could sort out / their destinies fairly freely" (*S*, 72). These statements seem to testify to an Emersonian faith in an inherent self-structuring that operates in the spontaneous and free-flowing. (Such self-structuring appears, in the view of *Sphere*, to be present both in the workings of the world and in the unfolding of the poem itself.) The primary danger, as Ammons sees it, is not that of a poem turning formless, chaotic, going "to pieces" (*S*, 33), but the creation or exhibition of structures that is accomplished through an excessive paring away (*S*, 71).

To be sure, there is a counteremphasis to all this in the poem.

Ammons speaks of the need to combine with the female "pudding" (a play on pudenda) the male principle of the rational, formed and defined (*S*, 75). He is drawn to distinctions and boundaries. He refers favorably to "clarity" and "identity" (*S*, 13), expresses a desire to "give everything a course" (*S*, 52), to arrive at a network "moved forward by a controlling motion, design, symmetry" (*S*, 58).[14] All in all, however, we find in *Sphere*, this "form of a motion," that the principal stress, as elsewhere in Ammons, falls more on motion than on "controlling." The poem is drawn to liquids that overpower structures or exist outside them (*S*, 60, 72) or to "interpenetrations" (a recurring term) that dissolve boundaries.

As was suggested at the beginning of this chapter, the focus on the motion of a linear mode derives from the desire for freedom and inclusiveness. An *a priori* commitment to something more ordered or shaped would be intolerably constricting, choking the pulse: "the only bearable / fence is the continuum" (*S*, 38). Here "continuum" appears to mean the undifferentiated flow of phenomena. But the poem itself is similarly defined, as the "continuum of the omnium-gatherum," which gets "as much being out of motion / as motion out of being" (*S*, 29).

While the fixed stanzaic form of *Sphere* might be regarded as a minor specimen of the sort of restriction the poem rejects, it is seen otherwise, not only as a passive device to accommodate whatever comes its way, but as the active instrument of an omnivorous consciousness. Just prior to its designation as the log against which the stream flows, the stanza is called a "maw [which] can grind / up cancers and flourish scarfs of dandelions" (*S*, 28). A kind of fusion of active and passive occurs in a passage where Ammons says the "abstract poem . . . / . . . acquires a skeleton to keep it here" (*S*, 71). It is plain that he regards *Sphere* as such a poem (in the course of it he designates himself as an "abstract poet" [*S*, 69]), and "skeleton" appears to be another reference to the poem's stanzaic form, which provides the one constant element in a work that is continually leaping about or meandering. Although an element of structure, the "skeleton" is made to undergo a "jangling dance [that] shocks us to attend the moods of lips, / the liquid changes of the spiritual eye" (*S*, 71).

While Ammons can adopt a modest tone in speaking of his poem, calling it a "waiting amusement" (*S*, 30) or his "magnum hokum" (*S*, 77), he also makes large claims for it. At one point, such a claim is simply part of a blanket endorsement of all things: "I go / on the confidence that in this whole magnificence nothing is / important, why should this be, yet everything is, even this / as it testifies to the changing and staying" (S, 46). But he can also declare that the abstract poem is "integration's grandest, most / roving whale," and compares it to the god Enlil (S, 71). In an obvious echo of Stevens (whom we also find making both small and great claims for his poems), Ammons says "if truth is colorless, fictions / need be supreme, real supreme" (S, 36). By this he appears to mean that if the ultimate is beyond our senses and apprehension, or alternatively, if it leads to nothingness, we need the artifacts of the poet to exhibit compellingly the graspable structures or patterns of the world in order to reconcile us to our place in it (this interpretation is based on my sense of the poem as a whole). His hopes are "for the shining image of nothingness within which / schools of images can swim contained and askelter" (S, 69).

Sphere repeatedly refers to "nothing" or "nothingness," thus echoing *Hibernaculum.* Like that work, *Sphere* is able to see nothingness as the source of possibility and plenitude (see sections 5, 150), but also as the emptiness to which we are brought by death. However, there is an additional, especially interesting meaning given to "nothingness" by *Sphere,* which is peculiar to this poem. That meaning has to do with the operations of the mind.

The term "mind" itself recurs throughout the poem, and mind may be said to function as the protagonist or hero of *Sphere,* which speaks of "mind's radiant works" (S, 25). In referring to the "radiance" that is produced in the making of a symbol, Ammons calls it "the simple result of / the categorizing mind: the mind will forever work in this way, / and the spiritual, the divine, always be with us" (S, 39). (We have here symbolist portentousness in curious combination with matter-of-factness.) In a related passage, Ammons speaks of "joy's surviving radiance" in a "moment of consciousness" (S, 41). Adopting at one point what seems to be the notion of a communal mind, he says that if one "adds a point of light" to it, this "lodges . . . a preserved energy, ever able to give energy off, / a great peculiarity, the only immortality known" (S, 22).

Enormous power, then, is attributed to mind, at least provisionally. The poem speculates that perhaps it "can wear out the earth" (S, 20), meaning, presumably, that in its operations mind can arrive at formulations that will cover all of earth's phenomena. *Sphere* goes on to speak of "interestingly inexhaustible quandaries," but these are things the mind "has come up with" rather than being properties of the observed world (S, 21). So that mind is here celebrated as creator of either formulas or connundrums. Reminding us of Emerson, Ammons attributes to mind a faculty that is "small, but masterful in the face of size and / spectacular ramification into diversity" (*S,* 42). Mind acrobatically rides a "cycle," moving from a sense of the One to a sense of the Many (*S,* 69). In one of the poem's finest passages, mind heroically rises above mere contentment in order to gain a perspective on its situation, a process that may involve its contemplating apocalypse:

> . . . the mind, a periscope
> in the perilous scope, rises from comforting immersions in
>
> what sways good and feels fine, the plush indulgences like
> ledges or canyon scarps rimmed with spring's finery of bush,
> the creams and jellies of reverie, and looks abroad for a
>
> reassuring scope to sweetness or for the oncoming, if
> distant, catastrophe that will return it to the pudding
> of change, the mind's own describing and roving fire
>
> drowned from shapening. . . . (*S,* 67)

Here, the mind's fire is in danger of being quenched, a liquid element its antagonist. But in earlier passages, mind (or imagination) is strikingly imaged in terms both of fire and liquid, and is viewed not as subject to destruction but itself a destroyer. In one such place it is described as "burn[ing] up or dissolv[ing] the day's images" (*S,* 53). Here this consuming process is seen as necessary if we are not to be overwhelmed by the proliferation of experience. Yet in another passage, as if afraid that such a process can be carried too far, Ammons says "let's . . . grab a few things from the flood, / from the imagination's burning everything up . . ." (*S,* 62). Considering these passages together, one deduces that Ammons is not distinguishing between the rational and imaginative modes of mind, but focusing consistently on mind's capacity to order and abstract from experience. While he may display pride, even hubris, in celebrating mind's operations, its capacity for "burning" or "dissolving," he is appalled by that very capacity: "one terror mind brings on / itself is that anything can be made of anything . . . / . . . the mind making things up, making nothing / of what things are made of" (*S,* 61). Here is the significance of "nothing" peculiar to *Sphere.*

It can be said that as the poem unfolds, we find Ammons, like

Milton's Satan, praising the power of mind to create its own place. But at the same time, Ammons feels something deeply wrong about thus dismissing creation as it exists, a given, a thing independent of mind's liquefying and arsonous acts. (Stevens shows a similar conflict.) That is to say, the celebration of mind works against Ammons' naturalistic piety, his appreciation of the world's structures and processes. Perhaps there is self-admonition in his asking "the mirrorments, astonishments of mind, / what are they to the natural phenomena" (S, 30).

This expression of a reverence for creation is part of the strong religious strain of the poem. Again and again in reading the work, one encounters a religious vocabulary, references to a "god" or "gods," the "most High," "He" or "Him," "grace," "prayer," "spirit," being "saved." A few of these references warn us not to conceive of divine force in anthropomorphic terms or to think of the sky as our ultimate home or to hunger after pure essence. But the bulk of such terms serves to invest the workings of the world with the quality of the charged and numinous, a quality making for appreciation, awe, astonishment. Ammons conceives of "true service" as a celebration of a "bountiful" He (S, 51).

In two or three places, the poem may be said to attempt a synthesis of its praise of mind and its reverence for the created world. The "gods," Ammons says, alternately come and go. (If they seem gone now, that is just a temporary condition.) This alternation has to do "with / the way our minds work." So that, in the passage in question (S, 48 - 49), the sense of divinity stands poised between being something that comes to us from without and something that is an emanation from ourselves. A similar ambiguous positioning is effected in another section of the poem, cited earlier, where radiance, mystery, and "the source of spirit" are seen as issuing from symbols, the making and effect of which are "the simple result of / the categorizing mind." The mind will forever work this way; consequently, "the spiritual, the divine [will] always be with us" (S, 39). But what would seem to be a pure humanizing of spirit and mystery is immediately tipped toward something beyond the human: "in the / comprehensiveness and focus of the Most High is the obliteration / total that contains all and in that we rest" (S, 39).

Perhaps the most significant fusion of mind and the divine occurs when Ammons tentatively suggests that being saved lies in so coming

> . . . to know
> the works of the Most High as to assent to them and be reconciled
> by them, so to hold those works in our imaginations as to think
>
> them our correspondent invention, our best design within the
> governing possibilities: so to take on the Reason of the Most
> High as to in some part celebrate Him and offer Him not our
>
> flight but our cordiality and gratitude. . . . (S, 41)

From this fusion of the Creation and imagination comes the "moment of consciousness" in which is located "joy's surviving radiance." That moment is one in which we prize the very thing that in the act of realizing itself consumes us, "the greatness that rolls through / our sharp days, that spends us on its measureless currents" (S, 41). Mind is given the privilege of contemplating, at least in moments, that process whose enactment includes the mind's dissolution. Ammons asks if we can "bend" to accept such a position, then seems to indicate that we can, although such bending is interestingly followed by a passage which speaks of the mind's power to create "bends," meaning its ability to order experience (S, 42). Thus, Ammons has followed an apparent acquiescence to mind's fate with a celebration of mind's force. But the impulse to have the mind accept and praise the great ongoing forces of the universe is a strong one in the poem. Ammons declares:

> . . . when you come
> to know the eternal forces realizing themselves through form
> you will need to lay on no special determination to assent
>
> to what demands none. . . . (p. 36)

There is a touch of irony here, but basically an acceptance.

The self need not feel dwarfed by its sense of the immensity in which it is located. Adopting a view very much like that of Whitman in *Song of Myself*, Ammons conceives of each of us as standing in "the cone of ages . . . / . . . each of us peak and center" (S, 32). Two Ammons terms that are essential to his consideration of the One and the Many are here casually joined to glorify the self (and see S, 12). "Motion," another key term, and one prominent in *Sphere*, also makes an appearance that enhances the self, serving to

join it with the world in harmonious union. In answer to the question of "how to be saved: what is / saving," Ammons replies:

> . . . come to know the motions with what rightness, accuracy,
> economy, precision they move and identify the motions of the
>
> soul with them so as to find the self responsive to and in
> harmony with the body of motions. . . . (p. 34)

Note the syntactical ambiguity in this passage. "Identify" can be
read as part of a compound imperative ("come to know . . . and
identify") or as part of a compound indicative ("move and identify") of which the subject is "motions." This ambiguity, assigning
the act of identifying both to an implicit "you" and to "motions,"
enacts the fusion of self and world that the passage is concerned
with. The rightness of the physical operations of Creation is seen as
extending to and incorporating the operations of the self. The
motions of the one mesh with the motions of the other, though only
through what seems to be a willed, tautological process.

Another, more satisfying version of the harmonious placement of
the self in the universe occurs later in the poem:

> . . . we are not half-in and
>
> half-out of the universe but unmendably integral: when we
> move, something yields to us and accepts our steps . . .
>
> . . . .
>
> . . . we move into the motions with our tiny oars: there
> are seas not oceans but invisible seas: they sustain,
> they drown, but the abundance, the intricacy and dispersion,
>
> is glorious. . . . (S, 43 - 44)

As the human miniscule joins up with the macrocosm here, the image of the tiny oars conveys a sense of ludicrousness and pathos as
well as one of significance and enlargement. The conception of this
passage, conscious of destruction as well as maintenance, is richer
than the earlier flat assertion of the correspondence of self and
world.

We have in the tiny oars dipping into the seas one of a series of
water images generously scattered through *Sphere*. Such words as

"waves," "tides," and "currents" are used to characterize not only universal processes but the experiences of the self as well, in a further joining of mind and world. A particularly prominent and important strain of the poem's water imagery consists of instances of *floating*. This action, in one form or another, makes over a dozen appearances in *Sphere*. In the course of the work it becomes attached to the self, matter, the earth, and the poem. It is associated with ease, well-being, release, inclusiveness, achievement, radiance, vision. As such, *floating* can lay claim to being a central, honorific term of the poem.

It registers with special force because of its contribution to the tone of the very last section of *Sphere:*

> to float the orb or suggest the orb is floating: and, with the
> mind thereto attached, to float free: the orb floats, a bluegreen
> wonder: so to touch the structures as to free them into rafts
>
> that reveal the tide. . . .

The passage continues with "we're gliding: we / *are* gliding: ask the astronomer, if you don't believe it," and the poem concludes "sew / my name on my cap: we're clear: we're ourselves: we're sailing" (*S*, 79). "Float," both in itself and through its reinforcement by "gliding" and "sailing," helps produce here an effect of climax in the form of a sense of euphoria. The quality of the earth's movement through space becomes translated into the final mood of a poem whose own stanzas might be considered "rafts / that reveal the tide."

This ending may be seen as of a piece with the religious strain of *Sphere*. But it goes counter to much else in the work, counter, indeed, to the original notion of the linear mode. Despising, as indicated earlier, "little rondures," Ammons produces the impression at the end of *Sphere* of having created a grand rondure, a resolved whole, a large filling out of his title, a roundedness which is at once his image of the earth and the poem itself. The notion of the linear mode as an ongoing procedure, which is not to be rounded off, seems to have been put aside. (*Hibernaculum*, otherwise very similar to *Sphere*, appears determined to conclude on a note of the arbitrary and casual.) Earlier in *Sphere*, after Ammons had called "for a form to complete everything with! orb," he had offered instant resistance to this desire for completion by saying "but this is

the / procedure" (S, 38). Also, just about at the exact midpoint of
the poem, he claimed he did not "want shape," that he would have
"water muscles bending streams (recurrences of / curvature)" (S,
45). Such recurrences may be figured as arcs, a kind of shape but
one distinctly less imposing than that of the sphere (compare Ammons' settling for such a modest shape in "The Arc Inside and
Out"). Yet the poem's ending, together with its title (it was originally called only *The Form of a Motion*), in effect lays claim to a grand
shape. The work may be said, in the last analysis, to conceive of
itself as an example of what it had seemed originally to reject,
"great procedures." Such procedures it defined as moving toward
inclusiveness, but "when they / have everything they have nothing,
an all-ness of identity / and no effect, a calm, resolved effect" (S,
50).

The sense of resolution at *Sphere*'s end is questionable on two
counts. For one thing, it presumes an increasing harmony of the
diverse parts of both this country and of the world, a reconciliation
of the One and the Many in social and political terms. The stanza
immediately preceding the final section speaks of "a united,
capable poem, a united, capable mind, a united capable / nation,
and a united nations! . . . / . . . seeking the good of all in the
good of each" (S, 79). Here, as in *Tape for the Turn of the Year*,
Ammons makes a presumption about the state of this nation and of
the world that many of us cannot share. Moreover, the euphoric
character of *Sphere*'s concluding section seems to have left behind
the troubled apprehension of things found a few pages earlier in the
poem:

> to be small and assembled! how comforting: but how perishable!
> our life the tiny star and the rest, the rest: this extreme
> flotation (it and us) this old, inconstant earth daily born
>
> new into thousands of newborn eyes—proceeding by a life's
> length here and there, an overlapping mesh of links proceeding:
> but, for me, turning aside into rust, reality splintering the
>
> seams, currents going glacial and glassy with knowledge, the
> feared worst become the worst: meanwhile, once again the world
> comes young, the mother follows her toddler around the cafeteria
>
> and can't see him her eyes so keeping in touch with the admiring
> eyes of others: (the old mother, thin-white, thick-jawed, feels
> her way, but barefooted, out to the mailbox: nothing: all

the fucking finished, all the sweet, terrifying children grown
up and blown away, just the geraniums in the tire watered
every day, fussed at, plucked:). . . . (*S*, 73)

Here the earth's "proceeding" (another recurring term in *Sphere*, a
variant of "procedure," and associated with mental, poetic, and
natural processes) does not harmoniously include Ammons or float
him as he is floated at poem's end. He is split off, isolated by the
"but, for me" passage. While the emergence of new life and mater-
nal pride constitute a large part of the proceeding here, so do aging
and inevitable isolation—the poem at this point is true to all of
these. Moreover, the lines quoted are framed by considerations of
"freezing gulfs of / darkness," as well as by a reference to the poet's
daily morning look "into the bottom of my grave" (*S*, 72, 73). (His
response to this last is to "proceed," but that seems a desperate,
personal undertaking, a *counter*movement to the larger proceeding
he has invoked.) The gulfs of darkness are linked by the poem to
acute personal losses in Ammons' life, losses that are permitted only
shy, minimal appearances in *Sphere*, but that are indubitably there.
(The particular example in the "gulfs" passage is the death of a
younger brother.)

The poem's final image of its maker and of the earth, floating,
gliding, sailing, fails to acknowledge sufficiently such materials (we
are given only the reminder "we must get off"). The concluding
section of *Sphere* floats free of at least some strains of the poem,
drawing solely on Ammons' sense of wonder and his belief in the
rightness of the universal currents. (Floating may be thought of as
the sensation produced by currents conceived of only as beneficent,
rather than "glacial and glassy.") I hesitate to quarrel with a
passage that has so much pleasure in it and that gives so much
pleasure, a passage that has been at least partly earned. But there is
a gap between it and the full range of feeling and conception
manifested in the work as a whole.

I have already noted that *Sphere* considers the possibility that
"the mind can wear out the earth" (*S*, 20). Reconsidering this, the
poem says that if it happens "there are still shenanigans left in / the
lingo" (*S*, 27). The wording of this in itself testifies to Ammons'
delight in his medium as well as to his confidence in it. Language,
inexhaustible, is always available, to sport with as well as think with.
Ammons' use of it in *Sphere*, as in other works, is marked by exuberance, evidenced, for example, by the pell-mell beginning of the
poem with its linking of the sex act to mental activity, and its treat-

ment of thought as an epistemological drama, rendered through
metaphors of hunting and eating. Other manifestations of *Sphere's*
verbal shenanigans are its punning (for example, "the / rightest
mind is shadowed by leftovers' dark carriages" [S, 22]), its burst of
internal and cross rhyme (section 110, S, 59), its rendering of the
large or grand in terms of the homely (for example, "bet on the
void" [S, 20], "the skinny seat on infinity" [S, 38]). This last is part
of the central verbal feature of *Sphere* (one it shares with *Hibernaculum*): its wide-ranging vocabulary, its habit of moving freely
among different levels or areas of diction, appropriating the formal
and the colloquial, the abstract and the concrete, the common and
the technical, the elevated and the lowdown. (Ammons' drive
toward inclusiveness takes in the English language.) The poem,
then, not only jumps from subject to subject, but darts from diction
to diction. If the notion of *continuum* operates explicitly in *Sphere*
to designate the unbroken flow of things, it operates implicitly in
the poem's vocabulary. That is, the whole of the language as it
presently exists is treated, in effect, as a single entity. (While Whitman, who is mentioned several times in *Sphere*, may be seen as a
forerunner of Ammons' practice, the poet who is perhaps closest to
him in this respect is the later Auden.) To put the matter another
way, just as the variegated surfaces of the earth are seen as coming
together in a sphere, the different subsets of English words are
handled as parts of a unified whole, to be drawn on anywhere and
everywhere by the poet.

In addition to lines already quoted, the following passages from
Sphere demonstrate its verbal amalgamations:

                    . . . we all approach the fine, our

skinny house perpetual, where in total diminishment we will
last, elemental and irreducible, the matter of the universe:
slosh, slosh: vulnerability is merely intermediate: beyond

the autopsy and the worm, the blood cell, protein, amino acid,
the nervous atom spins and shines unsmirched. . . . (S, [11] - 12)

                    . . . from implacability and

quandary we make shabby or golden peace: pain at the end will
move us like a willing rocket away: short of the cycle of
the natural ongoing is the human, a stream broken, bent,

stalled, re-begun that began back with the first transmissible
molecule and is sticking to time and motion still. . . . (*S, 22*)

. . . ardency is a

calf, butting and guzzling, let free to the cow: a luminous
saint reeling in the heights of objectless desire: hornets
after rain splitting out for lit flies: my heart shakes,

my eyes concentration's flames, you my attention, absolute:
dust travels, gets up into the wind's limbs and through
stirrings and catchments makes itself available to new

coherences, settles out, for example, carrying in microscopic
branches paramecium, virus, germ to damp stayings,
boom bloomings, gets going to return: leaves nothing lost. . . . (*S, 37*)

Such language expresses a sensibility in constant movement, widen-
ing and narrowing its focus, altering its tone, jumping from the
trivial to the grand, incorporating vision and verbal play. What was
predicted for mind in *Hibernaculum,* its eventually becoming
another earth, is seen in *Sphere* as a *fait accompli* (though in truth it
had arrived at the predicted condition even in *Hibernaculum*); it is
described as "many sided, globe-like, / rich with specification and
contrariety" (*S, 58*). Such, at least, is the mind of *Sphere,* working
strenuously through its storehouse of language to do justice to the
forms and flux, the shapes and flow of our earthly life, matching
them with the rich spectrum of its expressiveness.

CHAPTER 8

Conclusion

"EMERSON," a work found in Ammons' second most recent book, *Diversifications*, may be read as a look back to his beginnings, an explicit recognition by him that he needed "to get . . . down," that is, to make fuller contact with the concrete actuality of earth than he had been able to achieve in the early poems. *Ommateum*, whether evincing alienation or acceptance, had reduced the world to thin, stylized components, fitted too easily to the self's allegorical questings.

Beginning with *Expressions of Sea Level* and continuing thereafter, Ammons has succeeded in opening his poetry to the particulars of the world, allowing them to fill up the space traversed by his mind's flights. His sense of the world's invisible but inclusive configurations and currents is rooted in his apprehension of the small and visible. In "Off" Ammons says his "eyes' / concision shoots to kill," and in *Essay on Poetics* he claims "I think what I see" (p. 298). These statements point up his thirst for and dependence upon the prehension of the formed, the embodied. Harold Bloom has rightly noted that wind has given way to water as the dominant element in Ammons' poetry.[1] This displacement of an invisible element by a visible one is part of Ammons' commitment to the world of appearances. He honors that world, as did Whitman, Stevens, and Williams. A poem that sees a correspondence between water's motions and Ammons' own is called "Appearances," and in "Currencies" Ammons compares himself to "brooks, breaking over falls, / escaping with the silver of seeing."

But for all his openness to the world of appearances, Ammons has desired something beyond its pell-mell of particulars. Science has afforded him a way of locating these particulars in a series of patterns and processes. Such location has undoubtedly given him satisfaction. But he has wanted to get beyond this too, reaching for a sense of unity, a clarifying apprehension of the whole of things.

160

When such a quest is not qualified or questioned, but simply affirmed, it tends to return Ammons' poetry to its earlier allegorical or abstract character and leaves us looking at the experience from the outside, as in "The Unmirroring Peak," whose title designates a mountain in the mind, beyond change. It is the Ammons of such poems, longing for unity, vision, transcendence, the sublime, who seems to appeal most to Harold Bloom. Focusing on this Ammons, Bloom ignores or subordinates the humor, linguistic shenanigans, intellectual play, and delight in the concrete that figure so prominently in Ammons' work. At his best Ammons is as likely to be wry as rapt. His roving eye, often taking as target the modest particulars of the world, makes for a roving mind that does not consort well with the fixedness, elevation, and sense of ultimacy that his quest for transcendence or unity involves. In much of his work, Ammons seems to have implicitly endorsed Emerson's contention (in "The Poet") that "the quality of the imagination is to flow, and not to freeze."

Such flowing is what Ammons has attempted to maintain in his linear modes. To immerse in and enjoy this flowing the reader must be willing to forego the satisfactions of tracing an overall structure, and focus instead on the pleasures of texture. He must be willing to give up what D. H. Lawrence called the poetry of "Perfected bygone moments, perfected moments in the glimmering futurity," and accept instead "the poetry of the immediate present," the poetry of "mutation . . . haste, not rest, come-and-go, not fixity, inconclusiveness, immediacy . . . without dénouement or close." Lawrence cites Whitman's works as an example of such poetry. The spirit of Lawrence's remarks can be found in Charles Olson's notion of "Composition by Field" and in Robert Duncan's recognition of the possibility "that one might concentrate upon the sound and meaning present where one was, and derive melody and story from impulse not from plan."[2]

What can be seen as operating in these conceptions and particularly in Ammons' linear modes is a democratization of perception and of consciousness, a putting aside of restrictions or priorities. That which enters one's field of perception or thought is entitled to a place in the work at hand. This suggests another way of looking at Ammons' use of the colon. That mark is a sign of equivalence. It works against a sense of subordination, selection, priority, or hierarchical structure. Its repeated use gives us, instead, a series of equals.

There is a further democratization at work in Ammons' eclectic vocabulary. He has freely mingled varying levels or kinds of English. Out of the Many of the language, he has created, getting past the stylistic fragmentedness with which he began, a One, his medium. For all its variety it coheres, a United States of language. Despite their waywardness, and disconnected as they may be at any given point, his linear modes also cohere, pondering particular themes. As with the flow of things, which, in his view, produces a series of patterns and forms, so with those long poems, whose materials crystallize out in local continuities and cross-referential passages to register Ammons' preoccupations, conferring the identity that consists of "what / [he] can't keep [his] mind off." The local clusterings serve as islands in the flow. We can temporarily rest on one, but must then push off for another.

These linear modes record the flow of a mind continually thinking. Ammons sees, but *thinks* what he sees, doing so in virtuoso talk. The flow of this talk, the abundance of consciousness it gives us, can be astonishing, and promises that we shall get much more from this poet who, in mid-career, has already given us so much. Even as it honors the small and particular, that consciousness repeatedly establishes a large frame of reference, reminding us of our location on earth and in the cosmos. Such placement, as in Whitman, does not characteristically serve to diminish us; it is, rather, occasion for enthrallment and magnification. Continuing in the tradition of Whitman and Stevens, Ammons celebrates both the world and the self that perceives and ponders it.

Notes and References

Chapter One

1. See [A. R. Ammons], "Numbers," *Diacritics* 3 (Winter, 1973), [2].
2. For this, as for some of the other biographical data given here, see Nancy Kober, "Ammons: Poetry is a Matter of Survival," *Cornell Daily Sun*, April 27, 1973, p. 12.
3. Ibid.
4. "Numbers," [2].
5. Kober, "Ammons: Poetry is a Matter of Survival," p. 12.
6. Ibid.
7. The book sold sixteen copies in five years.
8. George Santayana, *Three Philosophical Poets* (Garden City, N.Y., 1953), p. 30.
9. Ibid., p. 20.

Chapter Two

1. In *Collected Poems 1951-1971* the titles of all the works that originally appeared in *Ommateum*, with the exception of "Doxology," are the same as the first lines. In *Ommateum* itself, again with the one exception, the poems were not assigned titles, only numbers.
2. Richard Howard, *Alone with America: Essays on the Art of Poetry in the United States Since 1950* (New York, 1969), p. 4.
3. Harold Bloom, *The Ringers in the Tower: Studies in Romantic Tradition* (Chicago, 1971), p. 258.
4. The being simultaneously alive and dead, the wasteland settings, the oppressive nature of the wind—these elements of *Ommateum* might be taken as echoes of Eliot's poetry.
5. This is an early work that did not receive book publication until *Briefings*.
6. See "Interview / A. R. Ammons," *Diacritics* 3 (Winter, 1973), 51. Also, note that Ammons' "A Poem is a Walk," *Epoch* 18 (Fall, 1968), 114 - 19, takes its epigraph from Lao Tse.
7. An interesting reversal of the situation in "A Crippled Angel" can be found in "Requiem." There, the speaker attempts to rise, and is "massacred" by angels. "Requiem" illustrates the persistence of the transcendental impulse in Ammons after his *Ommateum* period.
8. "I Came Upon a Plateau" furnishes another case of withdrawal from

the world, expressed in religious terms. While the poem lacks the humor I find in the one just discussed, the retreat seems to be derided.

9. The split between acceptance and rejection of the world in early Ammons is highlighted in *Collected Poems* by the juxtaposing of the last two poems listed as belonging to his 1951 - 1955 period, "This Black Rich Country" and "Look For My White Self." (These were not included in *Ommateum.*) The first embraces the human condition, the second envisions a purged, ghostly self singing on a mountain top.

10. I presume the foreword was written by Ammons. Its language may be said to adumbrate his imagery of "center" and "periphery," which will be discussed in Chapter 4.

11. In "Catalyst" the "iridescence of compound eyes" is explicitly assigned to insects.

12. For what might be called a transitional poem in this respect, see "The Wide Land," where the wind, after blinding the speaker, is apologetic.

13. See M. H. Abrams, "The Correspondent Breeze: A Romantic Metaphor," *Kenyon Review* 19 (Winter, 1957), 113 - 30, for a treatment of the way wind functions in romantic poetry. It is both destructive and creative there, but tends to be only destructive in early Ammons, with the exception of "In the Wind My Rescue Is."

14. In "Bridge" and *Summer Session* (p. 258), wind is associated with vision or poetic power.

Chapter Three

1. Such seems to be the suggestion, for example, of "Whose Timeless Reach," a suggestion which may help explain the departure from earth in "Some Months Ago," and which accounts for the *struggle* it takes to remain connected to the world in "With Ropes of Hemp."

2. See, as complementary to such poems, the connection between the eternal and nothingness, through the use of mud, in "Upright."

3. See "Lollapalooza: 22 February"; also, see *Hibernaculum*, sections 71 - 72 (p. 374).

4. In *Sphere* Ammons says "to be small and assembled! how comforting: but how perishable!" (S, 73).

5. In considering the qualifications of Ammons' attraction to form, it may be relevant to consider a work from *Northfield Poems*, "Zone." Here, after contemplating the realm of microscopic forms, on the one hand, and the domain of inclusive abstractions on the other, the speaker turns "strict with limitation, / to my world's / bitter acorns / and sweet branch water." In the poem the world of forms available to ordinary apprehension is accepted, but with a sense of its limits, and because there is no viable alternative. "Zone" is akin to Frost's "There Are Roughly Zones," and Ammons' title may be an acknowledgement of that kinship.

6. See also Marjorie Nicolson's treatment of the response to Newton by

eighteenth-century poets in *Newton Demands the Muse* (Princeton, 1966).

7. This comment, by Richard Howard, appears on the back cover of *Sphere*.

8. "Antennae to Knowledge," *Nation* 198 (March 23, 1964), 305.

9. "Note of Intent," *Chelsea*, nos. 20 - 21 (May, 1967), 4.

10. In *Sphere*, the pattern of leaves fallen under a tree is seen as "a shadow / of the universe! a record and perfect summary" (S, 70). The same poem declares "touch the universe anywhere you touch it / everywhere" (S, 72).

11. One of these is simply called "Motion." A number of other favorite terms show up as titles: "Mechanism," "Saliences," "Center," "Periphery," "Height," "One: Many." The significance of some of these terms will be dealt with in the next chapter.

12. "The Poetry of A. R. Ammons: Some Notes and Reflections," *Salmagundi*, nos. 22 - 23 (Spring - Summer, 1973), 286.

13. But it is possible to see an adumbration of the notion of form within flow in a phrase of "Doxology"—"fixed in rigid speed."

14. See *Tape*'s declaration that "anchorages / in motion are / solider than rock" (T, 124).

15. See *Sphere*'s statement that "motions are instances of order and direction" (S, 40).

16. The same phrase occurs in *Sphere*, p. 24.

Chapter Four

1. See Francis M. Cornford, *Plato and Parmenides* (New York, 1951), pp. 4ff.

2. See R. T. Wallis, *Neoplatonism* (London, 1972), pp. 61, 88.

3. M. H. Abrams, *Natural Supernaturalism* (New York, 1973), pp. 185, 186.

4. Ibid., p. 255.

5. Alfred North Whitehead, *Process and Reality* (New York, 1936), pp. 529 - 30.

6. Ammons indicated this in a letter to me (October 9, 1973), replying to certain queries I had made about his work.

7. That awareness includes at least some knowledge of Plotinus. In reading him, Ammons says in *Hibernaculum*, he found his mind "increased" (p. 370).

8. See Michael Kammen, *People of Paradox* (New York, 1973), passim.

9. This poem is not to be confused with Ammons' long poem *Sphere: The Form of a Motion*.

10. Was Ammons struck by this paradox in making his choices for *Selected Poems*? In the version of "In the Wind My Rescue Is" printed in that volume (p. 22), he eliminated the first stanza, which explicitly names the wind as a rescuing agent, and gave the piece the title "I Set It My Task."

11. For a poem that might be regarded as a counterstatement to "In the Wind My Rescue Is," see "Apologia Pro Vita Sua."

12. His ambivalence can also be illustrated by juxtaposing "High and Low," which regards descent and weeds favorably, with "The Wind Coming Down," which speaks of "terraces of mind" that "weedroots of my low-feeding [cannot] shiver."

13. In *Sphere* (p. 12), Ammons, somewhat playfully, indicates that the two sets of figures are indeed related.

14. Notice the use of "edge" in this passage, and see *Essay on Poetics*, which joins "edge" and "accident" (p. 306).

15. As indicated in Chapter 3, the poem finds the whole expressed in the part, but the means of that expression remain at the periphery.

16. Center may be unattainable because, as is sometimes the case with unity, there is nothing there. See *Essay on Poetics*, p. 299.

17. See *Tape*'s statement "when we solve, we're / saved by deeper problems" (p. 171).

18. This last phrase echoes "riddling through the underbrush" in "Thaw," which is an action ascribed to the wind. Putting the two poems together, we see another association in Ammons' mind between the wind and multiplicity.

19. "Object" is one of several poems where Ammons is self-critical because he has shirked strenuous enterprise, presumably of the imagination. See "Lion: Mouse" (whose closing lines echo "Object") and "Banking" (which strongly calls to mind Emerson's "Days"). In "Cut the Grass," the directive of the title is a comically trivial self-command.

20. It may be of interest to take note at this point of the Pythagoreans' Table of Opposites as it appears in Cornford's *Plato and Parmenides*, p. 6. One grouping of related terms includes the following: Limit (a quality associated with the One), Unity, Resting; the second set includes Unlimited (associated with multiplicity), Plurality, Moving. Emerson, in his essay on Plato, identifies unity with rest, diversity with motion.

21. I constructed this diagram shortly before coming upon the excerpt from *Sphere* printed in *Diacritics* 3 (Winter, 1973), 57 - [59]. There Ammons says: "for me . . . the one-many problem figures / out as an equilateral triangle (base: diversity and peak: unity)."

22. "Turning" may be read as endorsing any given form ("glass bead") as a center.

23. Contrast the use of "inside" and "outside" in this poem with their use in "Hymn." The notion of arduous quest, present in "Hymn," is rejected in "Arc."

Chapter Five

1. See Ammons' remarks on the country versus the city in "Interview," *Diacritics* 3 (Winter, 1973), 51.

2. "Path," which like "Gravelly Run" pictures the self as being per-

ceived by nature, rather than the reverse, has the human and natural converging, but only in terms of terrifying visions. The prefatory verse of *Sphere* explicitly finds the natural alien to the human.

3. I recognize that this intriguing poem is open to other interpretations, but I would like to register my strong disagreement with Harold Bloom's comments on it. He links it to a passage about a weed in "Saliences." Set at the seashore, that poem speaks of "a blue, bunchy weed, deep blue, / deep into the mind the dark blue / constant." Bloom cites this passage to illustrate his contention that in "Saliences" Ammons finds himself "in an astonishing equilibrium with the particulars [of the setting], containing them in his own mind by reimagining them there." He then goes on to say that "The weed and the mind's imaginative constancy are in the relation given by the little poem, *Reflective*, written just afterwards. . . . The whole meaning of [that poem] is in 'I *found*' [Bloom's italics], for *Saliences* records a finding, and a being found" (Bloom, *The Ringers in the Tower: Studies in Romantic Tradition* [Chicago, 1971], pp. 279 - 80). Apart from the dubious logic of this last statement, the weed of "Saliences" is far removed from the weed of "Reflective." The intensity and sensuousness with which the former is presented could not be more different than the measured pace and humorous contrivance with which we are given the latter. Is there really the "finding" of an "astonishing equilibrium" in "Reflective"? Ammons did not find the weed of that poem—he planted it.

4. See the description in "Storm" of trees, broken by wind and showing "the clean meat at the branch knot," as "clarified."

5. The decline of such a view of nature has been traced by Joseph Warren Beach in *The Concept of Nature in Nineteenth Century English Poetry* (New York, 1936).

Chapter Six

1. "A Poem Is a Walk," *Epoch* 18 (Fall, 1968), 114 - 15.
2. "Interview| A. R. Ammons," *Diacritics* 3 (Winter, 1973), 48.
3. "A Poem Is a Walk," 115.
4. In "Interview," 49, Ammons indicated that he could tolerate *some* talk about poetry.
5. Ibid. The idea that the motions of a poem end in no motion also appears in *Sphere*, p. 40.
6. "Mountain Wind," an uncollected poem (see *Diacritics* 3 [Winter, 1973], 54) also pictures the poet as a medium. See also "Poetics."
7. In *Tape* Ammons says "the resource, the / creation, and the end of / poetry is / language" (*T*, 177).
8. While it has an overall resemblance to "Thirteen Ways," "Configurations" actually comes closest to Stevens in the way its first stanza echoes section III of "Like Decorations in a Nigger Cemetery."
9. In section 7 the poem had said of the leaves: "out of so many / a

nestful missed the ground"; seen against the lines just quoted, this makes a connection between nest and poems, reinforcing the connection made in section 5 between nest and speech.

10. "A Poem Is a Walk," pp. 118 - 19.

11. This notion, of course, has appeared frequently since. Donald Hall has put the matter irreverently, saying "Poets tend to represent themselves either as detached craftsmen or as inspired, unconscious, mad mouthpieces" ("The Inward Muse" in *The Poet as Critic*, ed. Frederick P. McDowell [Evanston, 1967], p. 87).

12. See Stanley Burnshaw, *The Seamless Web* (New York, 1970), pp. 47ff.

13. T. S. Eliot, *On Poetry and Poets* (New York, 1957), p. 107.

14. Burnshaw, pp. 33 - 34.

15. Another less than exalted metaphor for poetry occurs in *Hibernaculum*, where Ammons compares it to soup, in what could be a parody of a metaphysical conceit (p. 357).

16. See Paul Valery's conception of a word in *The Art of Poetry*, tr. Denise Folliot (New York, 1961), pp. 55 - 56.

17. *Poetry* 102 (June, 1963), 202 - 3. Compare this with a remark Ammons made in an interview: ". . . I had been thinking of lines as a cascading, bouncing-back-and-forth effect that was really moving down the page instead of across. . . ." See Nancy Kober, "Ammons: Poetry is a Matter of Survival," *Cornell Daily Sun*, April 27, 1973, pp. 12 - 13.

18. See the passage in *Tape* where Ammons speaks of being "safe in . . . cages," singing joys, but then says "let me out of here" (p. 63).

Chapter Seven

1. *Tape* at first seems to be coming out of nothing except a desire to bring off a long poem. Eventually, however, Ammons indicates that "this ribbon of speech" is necessary, or else "the house" would be destroyed by pent-up passion (p. 13).

2. See pp. 35 - 37 and 192 - 95 of the poem. It may not be immediately obvious that these passages *are* addressed to the Muse, but I believe they should be read that way (additional readings are certainly possible).

3. Two of the three prose passages he quotes deal with the organization of biological entities (p. 314).

4. Ammons' use of this form in *Essay on Poetics, Hibernaculum, Sphere* and elsewhere, may owe something to the example of Stevens.

5. *Pray Without Ceasing* asks a question about "a 41-year-old man" (*D*, 97). *Summer Session*, published originally in *Uplands* as *Summer Session 1968*, specifies the poet's age as forty-two. This was Ammons' age in 1968.

6. The problem posed might also be regarded as an aesthetic one, that is, the keeping of shape and flow within a poem (see "Countering"), but I do not think that this is the primary meaning here.

7. A diction ranging from the formal to the childish can be found in Stevens, but he would never allow himself anything like "do do."

8. While I am convinced that this is the way Milton is being treated, that is, as an instance of mistaken structure-building, I am less sure of the poem's attitude toward Hegel. *Pray* raises the possibility that the "triadic Hegel" was basing his thought on his genitals, but I find Ammons' tone in considering this ambiguous (*D*, 84 - 85).

9. Also, note that the poem, near its conclusion, seems to characterize theorizing in what I take to be an *honorific* image, viz., "arising of skyscrapers, laws, / the high crystal-clear arising / of theory" (*D*, 97).

10. It should be observed that the poem appears to make a quick return to a felicitous condition when it speaks of opposing spheres coming together in a unity—but the phrasing applied to the unifying force, "reconciler and / putter to sleep," can be taken, at least partly, as derogatory, and is followed almost immediately by a quotation lamenting a lost religion.

11. Later, after some moralistic statements about "rampaging industrialists" and others, Ammons steps back from his poem to say "it's Sunday / morning accounts for such preachments, exhortations, and / solemnities" (p. 340). This takes note of what he has done but without destroying it.

12. I made the same assumption on p. 143 when I quoted the words "in order to hope he will / say something he means."

13. Here he is punning on the digging of a *well*, treated in the preceding section of the poem (7), which represents an attempt at ordering or clarification.

14. Ammons is something like Stevens' "Connoisseur of Chaos," who, even as he embraces the provisional, together with limited, small relations, a congeries of modest linkages, yearns for an all-encompassing order. But Stevens' imagined order is a relatively static one in that poem, whereas Ammons' assumes the form of an ongoing current or tide (see *Sphere's* final stanza).

Chapter Eight

1. Harold Bloom, *The Ringers in the Tower: Studies in Romantic Tradition* (Chicago, 1971), p. 283.

2. The materials from Lawrence, Olson, and Duncan, cited in this paragraph, can be found in *Poetics of the New American Poetry*, ed. Donald Allen and Warren Tallman (New York, 1973), pp. 70, 71; 147 - 58; 224, respectively.

Selected Bibliography

PRIMARY SOURCES

1. Poetry

Ommateum. Philadelphia: Dorrance, 1955.
Expressions of Sea Level. [Columbus, Ohio]: Ohio State University Press, 1964.
Corsons Inlet. Ithaca: Cornell University Press, 1965.
Tape for the Turn of the Year. Ithaca: Cornell University Press, 1965; New York: W. W. Norton, 1972.
Northfield Poems. Ithaca: Cornell University Press, 1966.
Selected Poems. Ithaca: Cornell University Press, 1968.
Uplands. New York: W. W. Norton, 1970.
Briefings. New York: W. W. Norton, 1971.
Collected Poems 1951 - 1971. New York: W. W. Norton, 1972.
Sphere: The Form of a Motion. New York: W. W. Norton, 1974.
Diversifications: Poems. New York: W. W. Norton, 1975.

2. Prose

"A Note on Prosody." *Poetry* 102 (June, 1963), 202 - 3. Ammons sees the stress in his poems falling at beginnings as well as endings of lines; this creates a pull "centrally down the page."
"Ginsberg's New Poems." *Poetry* 104 (June, 1964), 186. Finds "external reality . . . dictates Ginsberg's means." "The unity in Ginsberg's work is Ginsberg's search of [*sic*] unity. . . . The greater poem is possible when the poem is the sought unity."
"A Note on Incongruence." *Epoch* 15 (Winter, 1966), 192. Ammons defines a poem as an attempt to bring a "closer congruence" between "our non-verbal experience of reality" and its verbal reflection.
"Seven Books by Eight Poets." *Poetry* 108 (June, 1966), 196. Brief, scattered remarks on eight poets, including Robert Kelly and Mark Strand.
"Note of Intent." *Chelsea Review,* nos. 20 - 21 (May, 1967), 3 - 4. Ammons cites as his guide Wordsworth's contention that the poet will be able to assimilate the findings of science.
"A Poem is a Walk." *Epoch* 18 (Fall, 1968), 114 - 19. Quoting Coleridge, Ammons describes poem as nonlogical structure reconciling opposites, and develops what he sees as its characteristics through an extended analogy to a walk.

171

3. Interviews

GROSSVOGEL, DAVID I. "Interview / A. R. Ammons." *Diacritics* 3 (Winter, 1973), 47 - 53. Ammons discusses his conception of a poem, the nature of his relationship to Whitman and Emerson, his sense of apartness, his notion of history, the essential difference between country and city. Insists that he writes about *human* nature. Expresses interest in John Ashbery's work.

SECONDARY SOURCES

ASHBERY, JOHN. "In the American Grain." *New York Review of Books*, 20 (February 22, 1973), 3 - 4, 6. Includes review of *Collected Poems*. The fascination of Ammons' poetry is his struggle with the transcendental. He seems closer to "Action Painting" than the New York School of poets.

BERRY, WENDELL. "Antennae to Knowledge." *Nation* 198 (March 23, 1964), 304 - 6. Review of *Expressions of Sea Level*. Discusses Ammons' incorporation of scientific materials. Notes that the volume is focused on how things act rather than how they appear.

BLOOM, HAROLD. "A. R. Ammons: The Breaking of the Vessels." *Salmagundi*, nos. 31 - 32 (Fall, 1975 - Winter, 1976), 185 - 203. Finds intense war in Ammons' poetry between vision of mind as capable of taking "nature up into itself " and the belief that "nature can never be adequate to it." Insists that Ammons does not write nature poetry. He attains the Sublime in a void.

————. "A. R. Ammons: When You Consider the Radiance." In *The Ringers in the Tower: Studies in Romantic Tradition*. Chicago: University of Chicago Press, 1971. Places Ammons as descendant of Emerson and Whitman, but at the same time qualifies this connection. Pays special attention to "Corsons Inlet" and "Saliences," particularly the latter. Sees Ammons' imagination as relinquishing quest for unity and achieving a "painful autonomy."

————. "Dark and Radiant Peripheries: Mark Strand and A. R. Ammons." *Southern Review* 8 (January, 1972), 133 - 49. Ammons' portion focuses on *Uplands* and *Briefings*. Says "Emersonianism, the most impatient and American of perceptual traditions, has learned patience in the latest Ammons."

————. "Emerson and Ammons: A Coda." *Diacritics* 3 (Winter, 1973), 45 - 46. Dense piece, permeated by Bloom's jargon; says Ammons gives us a *daemonization* of Emerson.

————. "The New Transcendentalists: The Visionary Strain in Merwin, Ashbery, and Ammons." *Chicago Review* 24 (Winter, 1973), 25 - 43. Ammons resists his transcendental experience "in the name of a precarious naturalism," but some of his recent work is haunted by his old desire for unity with an Absolute. Like Emerson, Ammons is "a poet of the American sublime."

DAVIE, DONALD. "Cards of Identity." *New York Review of Books* 22 (March 6, 1975), 10 - 11. Includes review of *Sphere*. While suspicious of Ammons' "initial assumptions and governing preoccupations," found himself "enraptured" by the poem, won over by "the exuberance, the inventiveness." It is more logical for poetry that celebrates Becoming to use the inorganic form employed by Ammons than so-called organic forms.
DONOGHUE, DENIS. "Ammons and the Lesser Celandine." *Parnassus* 3 (Spring - Summer, 1975), 19 - 26. Discusses significance of wind and mountains in the poetry. Thinks Ammons evades history and other people. Favors the shorter poems over the longer ones. Finds Ammons impressive but unmoving.
HARTMAN, GEOFFREY H. Review of *Collected Poems*. In *New York Times, Book Review*, November 19, 1972, pp. 39 - 40. Ammons "subdues himself totally to *love of perception*, refusing all higher adventure." While describing him as a major American poet, Hartman thinks he "may be creating only an *objet trouvé* art."
HOLLANDER, JOHN. Review of *Briefings*. In *New York Times Book Review*, May 9, 1971, pp. 5, 20. Thinks of Henry Vaughan, Sir Thomas Browne, and D'Arcy Thompson as "some of Ammons' less obvious predecessors." His "work is probably to embody the major vision of nature in the poetry of our part of the century."
HOWARD, RICHARD. "A. R. Ammons." In *Alone with America: Essays on the Art of Poetry in the United States since 1950*. New York: Atheneum, 1969. Surveying Ammons' first five volumes, Howard finds in him a native American poetic impulse to immerse in reality and at the same time retain selfhood. Stresses Ammons' resistance to finitude, and talks of his predilection for littoral settings.
———. "A New Beginning." *Nation* 212 (January 18, 1971), 90, 92. This review of *Uplands* sees it reflecting the crisis of middle life.
———. "Auguries of Experience: The *Collected Poems*." *Boundary* 2 (Spring, 1973), 712 - 15. Claims Ammons invents a new prosody with each poem.
JACOBSEN, JOSEPHINE. "The Talk of Giants." *Diacritics* 3 (Winter, 1973), 34 - 38. Finds Ammons preoccupied with question of choices and limitations. Sees strong element of continuity in the poetry along with change and development. His works are antithetical to the culture which produced them.
KALSTONE, DAVID. "Ammons' Radiant Toys." *Diacritics* 3 (Winter, 1973), 13 - 20. Sees Ammons as maker of modern pastoral, defines him through comparisons to Whitman and Frost. Perceiver has replaced seer in Ammons, though "the ghost of the visionary is always there."
———. Review of *Uplands*. In *New York Times Book Review*, May 9, 1971, pp. 5, 20. Ammons recalls "romantic promises" but also confronts their disintegration, reminding us we are "intruders in nature." Comments on Ammons' titles.

KESSLER, JASCHA. "Exteriors." *Kayak*, no. 32 (July, 1973), 64 - 66. Strongly
negative review of *Collected Poems*. Sees Ammons as a lesser Thoreau;
finds him not as interesting and poetic as the scientific texts he draws
on.

KOBER, NANCY. "Ammons: Poetry is a Matter of Survival," *Cornell Daily
Sun*, April 27, 1973, pp. 12 - 13. Apparently based on an interview, this
article contains some important material, including statements by Ammons about his life and work.

MAZZARO, JEROME. "Reconstruction in Art." *Diacritics* 3 (Winter, 1973),
39 - 44. Discusses Ammons in relation to Emerson, Pound, Eliot,
Williams, Roethke, Thomas, Creeley. Admires *Tape*, but hesitates to
endorse those long poems that end "in process without vision."

MILES, JOSEPHINE. "Light, Wind, Motion." *Diacritics* 3 (Winter, 1973), 21 -
24. Describes Ammons' sentence structure, and defines his diction in
relation to that of other poets. Sees him showing an increasing "sense
of the general in the particular."

ORR, LINDA. "The Cosmic Backyard of A. R. Ammons." *Diacritics* 3
(Winter, 1973), 3 - 12. This valuable article talks of the split in Ammons between the Self (defined by language) and the Not-Self, his use
of the colon, his making motion a constant in his works, his humor and
irony.

PARKER, PATRICIA A. "Configurations of Shape and Flow." *Diacritics* 3
(Winter, 1973), 25 - 33. Follows Bloom in linking Ammons to Emerson
(as well as to Whitman and Stevens). Focusing on the figure of the circle, discusses the poems in terms of "center" and "periphery."

VENDLER, HELEN. "New Books in Review." *Yale Review* 62 (Spring, 1973),
412 - 25. Includes review of *Collected Poems*. Thinks Ammons finds
affluence in mind rather than nature. Offers capsule formulations of
Ammons' relationships to Hopkins, Stevens, and Williams.

WAGGONER, HYATT. "The Poetry of A. R. Ammons: Some Notes and Reflections," *Salmagundi*, nos. 22 - 23 (Spring - Summer, 1973), 285 - 94.
Compares Ammons to Emerson, and characterizes him as "a poet of
religious vision who is as wary of intellectualist abstractions as he is of
pious dogma."

Index

(The works of Ammons are listed under his name; the numbers in parentheses indicate the page on which it can be found in *Collected Poems* or, when preceded by a *D, Diversifications.*)

175